THE HERETICUS PAPERS

VOLUME II
of
The COLLECT'D WRITINGS
of
ST. HERETICUS

THIS COLLECTION of "Hereticus Papers" presents the humorous, sometimes satirical, and always pointed observations of "St. Hereticus" on theological, ecclesiastical, and political events and foibles of the years since *The Collect'd Writings of St. Hereticus* first appeared in 1964. Many of the pieces in the present collection were published originally in *Christianity and Crisis*. THE HERETICUS PAPERS will appeal both to previous St. Hereticus fans and to a new generation of readers who have not yet encountered his works. They will respond warmly to Hereticus' willingness to take on anything or anyone as he comments on the world about us. St. Hereticus is closely identified with Robert McAfee Brown.

The
HERETICUS PAPERS

(being Volume II of
"The COLLECT'D WRITINGS
of
St. HERETICUS")

To all of which is ANNEX'D
a RECENTLY Difcovered Mf.
ON
"THEOLOGICAL GAMEſMANſHIP: OR,
HOW TO DIſPOſE *of* LIBERATION THEOLOGY
IN EIGHT EAſY LEſſONS

Together with a piece of ORIGINAL REſEARCH
ON
"THE HERETICUS ICON"
BY
Karyn Kruſe

The whole INDEX'D for Eaſy Reſearching

Edited, with a Preface, by
Robert McAfee Brown

THE WEſTMINſTER PREſſ
Philadelphia, Pennſylvania
Anno Domini 1979

BOOK DESIGN BY DOROTHY ALDEN SMITH

First edition

Published by The Westminster Press®
Philadelphia, Pennsylvania

PRINTED IN THE UNITED STATES OF AMERICA
9 8 7 6 5 4 3 2 1

Library of Congress Cataloging in Publication Data

Brown, Robert McAfee, 1920–
The Hereticus papers.

Includes index.
1. Theology—Anecdotes, facetiae, satire, etc.
I. Title.
PN6231.T6B73   818'.5'407   79-10409
ISBN 0-664-24265-0

The book of Amos is very quotable.
None of the quotes make good bumper
stickers.

—*William Pannell*

I ought, therefore . . .

—*I. Kant*

CONTENTS

ECUMANIA

RECIPE: TAKE ONE PORTION OF RELIGION AND ONE OF POLITICS; MIX WELL

INSIGHTS FROM THE MILITARY WAY OF LIFE

FOIBLES OF OUR TIME
(*With apologies to James Thurber,* Fables for Our Time)

A NON-PROSE SECTION
(So described in deference to those who are fastidious about the use of the word "Poetry")

MISCELLANY
(Things That Didn't Fit Anywhere Else but Obviously Couldn't Be Left Out)

APPENDIX

PREFACE

IT is a heavy obligation to be literary executor for a saint. How is one to decide which pieces should be retained (the "essential" Hereticus); which should be discarded (as either unworthy, outdated, or libelous); which should be shortened or rewritten (many of Hereticus' earlier writings were sexist, a fact for which the initial essay in the present collection is offered in partial atonement); and which should be declared spurious (i.e., those for which nobody any longer wants to assume accountability)? One does not make such decisions lightly, particularly at a time when orthodoxy is on the rebound and heresy is looked on askance in many quarters where it was previously welcomed. This—it need hardly be said —is not a time To Retire From The Fray but a time To Act Boldly And Resolutely. A single criterion, therefore, has been employed in selecting materials for the present volume: *Anything that might give offense in any quarter was held to be, in principle, admissible*—"offense" being understood not in a nasty sense but in a genial sense, i.e., calculated to cut through pretentiousness not with a knife but with a smile. It is for others to say how well the criterion has been implemented. They surely will, for they always have.

The Collect'd Writings of St. Hereticus (of which the present work, *The Hereticus Papers,* is Volume II) included a lengthy monograph on the state of Hereticus research to the year 1964. It has been thought unnecessary to update this at the present time, the twentieth anniversary of the monograph (i.e., 1984) seeming a more propitious moment for whatever revisionist needs have accumulated over the double decade. There has, however, been important work done in the area of artistic and iconographic research, an area neglected in the original monograph since at that time the existence of iconography related to St. Hereticus was unknown. It is a pleasure to share with readers of the present volume the fullest analysis yet made of the icon, known appropriately, though perhaps redundantly, as "The Hereticus Ikon."[1]

A parenthetical reference was made in the second sentence, above, to the presence of sexist language. Would that the problem could be confined to a parenthesis. But it remains a problem in reprinting *any* literature from the recent or distant past. Sometimes the sexist references have been eliminated; at other times they have been accounted for by editorial comment in the footnotes.[2] But one set of words has consistently defied de-sexing, namely, composite terms such as "Gamesmanship" and "Observermanship." Surely the most hardened feminist will agree that a neologism like "Gamespersonship" loses something in transition. Consequently, in the case of such words, the old forms have been retained with apologies, pending the discovery of more adequate substitutes. Those who are still uneasy (or outraged) at the retention of "-man-" in the midst of these polysyl-

---

[1] This will be of particular use to those who employ audiovisual techniques in the training of the young.

[2] See footnote 3 for the formula employed to indicate when a footnote has been added by the Editor rather than the author.

labic concepts are invited to savor the possibility that the sins being described may exhibit shortcomings unique to the male of the species.

There remains only the question of the possible "datedness" of some of the papers. Serious attention has been devoted to this problem. In a few cases, inconsequential material has been deleted, especially when the passing of time had rendered it (a) obscure, (b) irrelevant, or (c) untrue. In a few other cases, explanatory footnotes have been supplied by the Editor so that the richly nuanced relevance of Hereticus' contemporaneity will not be lost on the uninstructed.[3] Occasionally, however, items that might initially have seemed appropriate to only one set of historical circumstances have turned out, upon examination, to be more apposite to the present era than could have been anticipated even by the luminous prescience of a saint. With only the slightest change of a name, a word, or a phrase, references to the Second Vatican Council (for example) or the Uppsala assembly of the World Council of Churches can be rendered appropriate for the upcoming Third Vatican Council[4] and all subsequent assemblies of the World Council of Churches.

There is a lesson in this for all of us: *the techniques remain constant; only the names and numbers of the players change.*

ROBERT McAFEE BROWN

September 31, 1978
Feast of the Maculate Assumption

---

[3]Footnotes by the Editor have the word "Ed." at the end of them in brackets, like this: [Ed.]

[4]I know something you don't know.

Acknowledgments

MOST of these pieces appeared at one time or another in *Christianity and Crisis.* The Editor is grateful to the journal for permission to reprint them in amended form. Most of the pieces were typed by Joyce Stoltzfus. The Editor is grateful to her for permission to reproduce them in unamended form.

Karyn Kruse not only contributed "The Hereticus Icon" but also created the line drawing immortalizing the ordination of Stanislaus Wienowski (Figure 47).

THE HERETICUS ICON

by Karyn Kruse

THE recent discovery of an icon of an obscure saint has lit a raging controversy in the fields of art and religion. Critics and theologians have been trying, with little success, to come to some conclusion about the work and its significance in the fields of theology and art criticism.

The piece that has touched off the controversy appears to depict one St. Hereticus.[1] O. Felix Culpa, the artist who is doing the restoration work on the piece, says that the saint was painted in tempera on a wood panel 38.5 × 29.0 cm. There is strangely no gesso background under the painting, indicating that the work is probably much older than earlier estimates have suggested. The painting is covered with several coats of varnish, as is usual in works of this type. Hereticus is depicted standing within pillars, under a pointed arch, behind a bookstand. He holds a pen in his hand, and a bumblebee[2] hovers near his right elbow. The significance of the bee has been disputed. Normally, the presence of a beehive or bee in Renaissance art signifies that the person de-

---

[1]One scholar, who requested that his name not be mentioned, suggested that the icon might be St. Boniface, but this hardly seems likely in view of the inscription "Scs HERETICVS" which appears on the icon.

[2]Of the genus *Bombus* and the family Apidae.

picted is a great orator, that he is, so to speak, "honey-tongued." It might also signify, as St. Ambrose suggests,[3] a type of virginity. Or it might suggest diligence or hard work. Unfortunately, none of these virtues seem in the least indicative of the character of St. Hereticus, as revealed to us in his writings. Thus it seems that either (a) we have the wrong St. Hereticus, or (b) the bee is being used in a new symbolic context, or (c) the artist squashed a bee on the painting and failed to clean it off. In support of hypothesis b, Vorschlung[4] suggests that the bee in the icon is not really a mere bumblebee,[5] but that it represents the kind of bee commonly found in bonnets. Unfortunately, the true meaning of the bee lies with the artist.[6]

Luckily, the symbolism of book and pen seems obvious, since all that is known of Hereticus is his writings. The nimbus, or halo, surrounding the head of the figure is perhaps one of the commonest of symbols, signifying holiness, or at least sainthood.

Generally it is safe to say[7] that icons[8] were mainly an art form of the Byzantine period, and later spread to Russia. Images of holy figures and saints were encouraged by the early church for the simple reason:

Segnius irritant animos demissa per aurem
Quam quae sunt oculis subjecta fidelibus.[9]

[3]Saint Ambrose, *De Virginitate*, Bk. I, ch. VIII.

[4]Erik Vorschlung, "Zur Frage die Symbolik dem Heretikusikon," *Studia Patristica*, 1967, XII:2, p. 375.

[5]Of the genus *Bombus* and the family Apidae.

[6]Assuming of course, that the artist is lying somewhere.

[7]It is generally safe to say almost anything if at first you take the precaution to amend your statement by saying "generally."

[8]We restrict our meaning here to small, two-dimensional panel paintings bearing the images of saints, the virgin, or other holy figures, as opposed to the larger original meaning of the term.

[9]Horace, *de'Arte Poetica*, Jerusalem: Habib B. Eerdmans Publishing Company, 1937, p. 153.

Yet, the Hereticus icon bears three distinctly non-Byzantine features: (a) the background is maroon, and not the traditional "nonrepresentational gold"[10] of most Byzantine art; (b) the lettering appearing above the right shoulder of the saint is obviously Roman style, not Greek, as in most icons;[11] and (c) the arch portrayed in the icon is pointed, a style that originated in northern France in the last half of the twelfth century[12] and never caught on in the south.

It has been suggested that the panel is not an ordinary icon at all, but was originally part of a polyptych. However, there are no hinge marks that would indicate this, and besides, Hereticus is rather an unlikely saint to be carried in procession,[13] and the piece is too small to be an effective altar decoration. Thus it seems that the piece is indeed intended to be used as an icon.

The style of the icon is, interestingly enough, quite similar to that of many illuminated manuscripts,[14] particularly in regard to the pose of the figure, the facial detail, and the saint's enclosure in pillars and arch. Also, it is remarkably flat, unlike Italian panels, which are usually carved in some way. Posthaste[15] suggests that the

---

[10]It has been suggested that the traditional gold background may be lacking because the vows of involuntary poverty taken by Heretican monks would make it impossible for the artist to purchase the gold needed for it.

[11]And the observer will immediately note that it completely omits the Schmerlhausen-Möllendorff Omicron.

[12]It is, of course, possible (though not likely) that the artist was a great innovator and invented the gothic arch long before it was used. This would account for the lack of other works by this artist, since innovators are less than popular members of most societies.

[13]See Monsieur J. Laplume de Matante, *L'histoire des hérétiques*, Paris & Barcelona, Rue Voltaire 94, 27 vols., 1909 ff.

[14]Notably the Otto III Gospels (ca. 1000), the Godescalc Gospels (781–783), and the St. Augustine's Gospels (late sixth century).

[15]Erwin Posthaste, "The Hereticus Debate," *Motive*, XXVII:1 (Oct. 1966), p. 31.

icon must have been painted by someone who specialized in the illumination of books.

Scientific methods of dating have so far been unsuccessful,[16] though there is great hope that eventually they will give us the answer to the riddle. At the present time, the best estimate, based on careful scholarship and historical and stylistic data (as presented in this paper), is that the icon must have been painted sometime before the year 1000 and sometime after the first half of the thirteenth century.

The Discovery of the Icon

The Hereticus icon was discovered during spring cleaning in a monastery in east central Minnesota. The origin of the piece is not known to the monks, though most scholars agree that it is not native to the United States, the country not having been discovered at the likely time of the painting of the piece. Schönburgher[17] suggests that since it was found in Minnesota it was probably brought from Scandinavia. The style, he admits, is not Scandinavian, but it might have belonged to a French or Italian monk who emigrated to Sweden to avoid fighting in the Crusades. Schönburgher is the first to admit that this theory is speculative, at best.[18]

Ankelgaard,[19] on the other hand, is convinced that the

---

[16]Data on the icon was fed into the Stanford University computer, but ever since a first-year sociology grad programmed it, all the computer has put out is life-size printouts of nude female figures.

[17]Emil Schönburgher, "Das Ikon Heretikus," *Zeitschrift für Kirchengeschichte*, XCVIII:3 (April 1968), p. 345.

[18]Sonovitch[20] claims that he admitted it first. This debate still continues.

[19]Søren Ankelgaard, "Heretikuus," *Svensk Teologisk Kvartalskrift*, IX:4, p. 283.

[20]Boris Sonovitch, "De Pravda vons Ikon," *Letopis Pechatnykh Proizvedenii Izobrazitel Novo Iskusstva*, XXXIV:3 (Sept. 1968), pp. 948ff.

icon is German, and was brought to Wisconsin from Germany. When the site of the monastery was moved from Wisconsin to Minnesota the icon traveled along, escaping detection by being hidden in material from the monastery's archives (which are still in such a state that even the curators can't say exactly where things are).

Research on Hereticus

Research on St. Hereticus, the man and his work, is sorely lacking. Most of the work done before 1964 has been covered in Robert McAfee Brown's introduction to *The Collect'd Writings of St. Hereticus.*[21] Not to be critical of Dr. Brown's scholarship,[22] there are nevertheless certain problems in his work that need to be aired. For example, on the very first page of his introduction[23] he states that Hereticus is not once mentioned in the following, otherwise fine, theological works:

T. Aquinas, *Summa Theologica* and *Summa Contra Gentiles;* J. Aquinas, *Zur Phänomenologie der Begegnung;* Wm. James, *Konzil von Trent;* and J.-P. Sartre, *Qui êtes-vous?*

Now, it is true that Hereticus' *name* is not found in these particular works, but how much more important is Hereticus' influence! For example, Gregory of Nyssa (ca. 335–395), in his *Oratio Catechetica,* ch. XXIV,[24] is obviously applying the teachings of Hereticus[25] when he says:

---

[21]Philadelphia: Westminster Press, 1964.
[22]These things have a way of backfiring.
[23]Brown (ed.), *op.cit.,* p. 1.
[24]Found in *Select Library of Nicene and Post-Nicene Fathers of the Christian Church,* Second Series, Vol. 5 (Grand Rapids, Mich.: Wm. B. Eerdmans Publishing Company), 1954.
[25]Hereticus, *Collect'd Writings,* Part Three: "Making the Bible Relevant" (Philadelphia: Westminster Press, 1964), p. 72.

". . . that so, as with a ravenous fish, the hook of the deity might be gulped down along with the bait of flesh . . ."

How much closer than this can one get to Hereticus' "Sportsman's Bible"?

Later in church history, we can easily see evidence of Hereticus' influence in the very 95 Theses that Luther is said to have posted on the church door. Theses numbered 24, 28, 31, 32, and others show distinct signs of Heretican influence.

Modern theologians are also showing signs of Hereticus' influence. There is known to be a passage in Paul Tillich's *Systematic Theology* that clearly echoes Hereticus' thought, and a team of scholars at the Heretican monastery is studying the work in an attempt to discover just what it is.

Yet, in all the volumes of theology that have been written, there is no mention of St. Hereticus. Not one footnote stands in tribute to this lonely scholar. And why? This author would like to suggest that while in true saintly humility Hereticus rarely signed his work, his brilliant mind lent its light in places where his name never shone. It is my contention that Hereticus used a pseudonym. Who but Hereticus could have written praises to Folly? It is my contention that Hereticus adopted, for humility's sake, the name of Desiderius Erasmus of Rotterdam, at least for a part of his work. I shall continue in pursuit of this theory and shall report any findings.

A Little Theology Goes a Long Way[1]

SIX ELEGANT PROOFS
FOR THE EXISTENCE
OF SANTA CLAUS

WHAT to talk about at the Christmas gatherings? Surely we must have something for the children. What more could we give them than a firm faith in the existence of the reigning deity of the culture religion of our nation, S. Claus, Esq.? If our faith is foundering, on what can we found it firmly? Surely, on reason, another reigning deity of our times.

The following text, if read firmly and assuredly to adults, can instill in them a new assurance which they (making the necessary translations) can then transmit to their offspring crying for belief in an era of unbelief. The only preparation needed is that a $5 bill be placed in the pocket or wallet ahead of time, for reasons that will (as the saying goes) become apparent.

After whatever initial pleasantries the occasion calls for, the substantive text may be read:

The existence of Santa Claus can be proved, and that in six ways:

1. The ontological argument. I have in my mind the idea of a Santa Claus than which no greater can be nor be

---

[1] All the way to p. 37.

conceived. He is a most perfect Santa Claus. He has an infinite number of toys. He gives to each child all that he or she asks, and more. He can move with the speed of light, or faster if necessary. He can negotiate all chimneys, from the widest to the narrowest. Indeed, it is easier for him to get down even the tiniest chimney than for a camel to go through the eye of a needle.

But such a Santa Claus exists not only in my mind but outside my mind as well, or else the idea in my mind would *not* be the most perfect Santa Claus, since it would lack one of the attributes of perfection, namely, existence. The very idea of "the most perfect Santa Claus" necessarily implies his existence.

Objection 1: Generations ago Immanuel Kant (note the name, Immanuel) said that he could imagine a perfect $100 bill in his pocket, but that did not mean that the $100 bill actually existed. There was no necessary transfer from idea to reality.

Reply to Objection 1: Kant's initial premise must be rejected as fallacious. No professor has ever had, let alone been able to imagine having, $100 in his pocket at one time. The invalidity of Kant's premise already threatens the validity of Kant's conclusion.

Further Reply to Objection 1: Pursuing Kant's point within a more realistic conceptual framework, I can imagine the existence of a perfect $5 bill in my pocket: it has a portrait of Lincoln, a drawing of the Lincoln Memorial, a serial number, and the signature of George Shultz. But does this idea of a perfect $5 bill in my pocket mean that I have an actual $5 bill in my pocket? No, said Kant.

But he was wrong. For when I reach into my pocket, I do indeed find within it a $5 bill.[1] This amounts to a

---

[1] Here the lecturer may employ actions suited to the text.

double proof, since empiricism has come to the aid of ontology, something rarely achieved elsewhere in the history of philosophical theology.

Thus we have, inverting the Kantian dictum, destroyed faith in order to make room for reason and even for empirical validation. As Anselm said so well, *Credo ut intelliclaus,* or "I believe, in order that the reality of Santa may be true for me."

2. The argument from a first clause. Let us shift from Anselmic back to Thomist presuppositions. As I look about the world, I am aware of the existence of many clauses: subordinate clauses, dependent clauses, sanity clauses, and so forth. Does the existence of any of these clauses assume the status of a self-explanatory phenomenon? Of course not. In every case we find ourselves involved in an infinite regress, which is no solution to the problem but only another way of stating it. And since the mind cannot rest content with an infinite regress, we are forced to posit the existence of a First Clause, itself unclaused.

And this all men[2] call Santa Claus, the holy or sacred clause.

The argument can assume *a second form,* arguing from effect to clause, e.g., from the effect (presents under the tree) to a First Clause who put them there. But this argument is already effectively present throughout our history as the clausmological argument.

3. The moral argument. It is well known that all persons can make moral distinctions. Sociological studies make abundantly clear that the moralism of our culture springs from a deep-seated belief in Santa Claus, viz.:

---

[2]The sexist language is that of Thomas, not Hereticus. [Ed.]

"Be good or Santa won't leave you any presents." Without this moral suasion, there would be no sense of right and wrong in human experience.

But there *is* a sense of right and wrong in human experience, since "it is well known that all persons can make moral distinctions" (see above). It must therefore be grounded in the objective reality of Santa Claus.

The argument can also be stated in the following manner: It is well known that the only thing upon which all church leaders are agreed is their disdain of "moralism." Without moralism there would be little or nothing for church leaders to combat. But if there were no moralism, then there would be no need for church leaders, as the very existence of church leaders could be questioned, since (to paraphrase Reinhold Niebuhr) if that which it exists to question can itself be questioned, then it can be questioned whether its own existence is or is not questionable.

The result is that without the existence of Santa Claus, and the moralism that proceeds from him, church leaders would no longer exist, save on the basis of falsehood, deceit, illusion, and fraud. Such a conclusion is unthinkable, and therefore will not be thought.

Alternative line of rebuttal: If Santa Claus does not exist, and this means that church leaders do not exist, such a price might be well worth paying.[3]

4. *The no-nonsense proof:* ". . . Doesn't exist? Hell, the whole American economy *depends* on him!"

5. *A series of proofs based on liberation theology:* There is one possibly damaging argument against the existence of Santa Claus that is offered *con mucho gusto* or, as liberation

---

[3]Here is a possible point for group discussion. [Ed.]

theologians might prefer to say, *con mucho gustavo*. The argument states that Santa Claus is the artificial construct of a bourgeois mentality, the product of a dominant theology concerned only to make sure that the rich get richer. At the very moment when the capitalist system began to break down, shortly after the advent[4] of the Industrial Revolution, Santa Claus was invented by the ruling class to provide what the system itself could no longer easily provide for everyone—surplus values. Santa became a kind of *Cleus ex machina* to keep the rich happy.

Note only a few of the decadent bourgeois capitalist imperialistic presuppositions inherent in the concept: (a) Santa visits only those with chimneys, a bare 7 percent of the world's population; (b) he has a whip, ostensibly for his badly exploited "eight tiny [*sic*] reindeer," but clearly meant to symbolize the shop stewards of the era when children were working twelve hours a day; (c) he smokes a pipe, symbol of a bourgeois comfort denied to the masses, filled with tobacco raised by underpaid workers to increase the bloated profits of greedy entrepreneurs; (d) instead of providing employment in overpopulated areas where it is needed, he moves his factories to the far north where he can exploit unorganized workers who have not yet been conscientized to appreciate the importance of labor unions, thus practicing a virulent colonialism that should have been stamped out long ago; (e) he employs only elves in his sweatshop, failing to conform to the minimal standards of an Equal Opportunity Employer.

In the light of all this (to invert Voltaire), "If Santa Claus existed, it would be necessary to destroy him." Clearly, the existence of Santa Claus would be disproved

[4]Note the clever play on words. [Ed.]

if the masses took up arms and destroyed him, since, according to the Philosopher, that which has ceased to exist cannot any longer be described as existing.

We thus have a *potential* disproof of the existence of Santa Claus, which could be escalated into an *actual* disproof (to employ the modalities of potentiality and actuality so dear to Aristotle) if action were undertaken by the masses, and if reflection were joined with action in *praxis*. Consequently (to put it in language the masses can understand), *the perpetuation of this praxiological possibility is continuously quantifiable.* In the words of the venerable Ernst Bloch, "If Santa does not yet not exist, he may one day not exist," although this form of the argument is clearly no more than a chip off old Bloch.

Fortunately, however, there is another way to attack the problem in which, by argument from similar presuppositions, one can prove the existence of Santa Claus even to the satisfaction of the Marxists. The proof starts from the undoubted fact that things are *difficult* for Santa Claus. Imagine having to fit into all those odd-sized chimneys; as Woody Allen would be the first to admit (and probably has), the cleaning bills alone would be appalling. So there is a real *struggle* in the life of Santa Claus, what our British cousins would refer to (in their characteristically sensitive intonation) as the "claus struggle." It is well known that for many years people doubted the existence of the claus struggle. But the recent researches of liberation theology have established, to the satisfaction of all, that there *is* such a thing as the claus struggle. Indeed, its marx are everywhere. Had René Descartes been a citizen of the Third World and had he written in Spanish (two easily entertainable assumptions), he would undoubtedly have formulated his famous statement to read *Lucho, luego soy* ("I struggle, therefore I am"), and described it as the quintessential statement of Santa Clausness.

Since there is indeed a claus struggle, as has already been shown, then there must be a claus. For, according to the Philosopher, if an entity exists, those separate parts of the entity must also share in the existence of that of which they are a part. Q.E.D.

If more proof were needed, it could be found in the clothing in which Santa Claus is invariably attired. For who are the proponents of the claus struggle? We know the answer to that: the reds. And what color does Santa Claus wear? We know the answer to that too: red. The coincidence is too striking, too full of perichoretic amplitude, to be the result of mere chance. It must therefore be a further variant upon, and corroboration of, the argument from design, based on the design of the very garb that Santa wears.

So much for the five ways of proving the existence of Santa Claus. But there is a final way, beyond way five. We might for convenience' sake call it way six, save that it would be more correct to denominate it (if we can do so without blushing) as way *sex*. It is:

6. The argument from sexuality. Let us immediately make clear, particularly in mixed company, that this is no invitation to prurient speculation, a fact concerning which St. Thomas himself would have been the first to breathe a sigh of relief.

It is a matter of considerable interest, not to say suspicion, that the question of the sex of Santa Claus has never, in any serious way, been the subject of critical reflection (let alone *praxis*, God forbid). It seems clear that there has been a conspiracy of silence over several centuries on this most delicate but infinitely important matter—the result (it is now clear) of a masculine-dominated literary and theological tradition from which it is now time to spring loose. Let us spring.

Why is it that before this moment no one has ever commented on the fact that we do not say and never have said "Saint Claus" or even "Sant' Claus," but have always and invariably used the feminine form "Santa Claus"? The "-a" ending is feminine in all Romance languages, as well as in the Latin from which they ultimately derive. We can allow for the natural elision that over the course of time would replace the original harsh "Sancta" with the smoother, more musically appealing "Santa," a linguistic adaptation of which even the immortal Dante would surely have approved, traditionalist though he was in so many other ways.

The linguistic evidence, in other words, conspires to suggest—nay, to establish—that Santa Claus was originally feminine, and that a nefarious attempt has been made to take the original verbal form and cover it over —attempt to smooth it, if you will—with a masculine corporeal form. But so great is the power of the word (*verbum,* as the scholars put it) that mere corporeality (even the massive corporeality of the Santa Claus of popular myth and legend) is not sufficient to destroy it.

Ergo: when we hear the base canard that "Santa Claus is dead," we can reflect that the only thing that has been destroyed is *our own conception* of Santa Claus, the way we have spoken of "him," the masculine images we have falsely and wrongfully imposed out of our cultural impoverishment.

Yes, Virginia, on one level there is no Santa Claus, and a good thing too. The Santa Claus of commerce is dead, that overweight and noxious male image of a vengeful provider, giving only to the good and withholding from the bad, instilling in children the fear of being passed over.

Freed now by the death of this distorted image, the true Santa Claus emerges unscathed by the petty speculation of human minds. May she assume her rightful place as the source of joy and hope, the guarantor of an open future.

ADVENTUROUS ADVERTISING
AND BIBLICAL BUTTRESSING:
A CHRISTMAS COLLATION

IF nobody else is ready to do it, Smith-Corona is ready to do it, i.e., "put Christ back into Christmas." Well, not Christ exactly, but St. Paul, who, if he is not Christ exactly (as he would be the first to admit), nevertheless comes closer than the rest of us.

Smith-Corona has given us a nifty Christmas advertisement, which itself should be clipped from the back cover of *The New Republic* and elsewhere, mounted in plexiglass and distributed widely as a Christmas gift, so perfectly does it grasp the spirit of the American Yuletide season.

In a scene redolent of Bethlehem, we confront a Mature Man (as the text will shortly assure us), sitting in an expensive chair, flanked by an expensive fireplace (walnut, or at least walnut veneer) and an expensive Christmas tree featuring dozens of expensive and unopened presents. On his lap is an expensive and opened present, none other than a Smith-Corona typewriter, and on his face is an ineffable smile, as though the beatific vision had just been vouchsafed to him. Apart from the words "Smith-Corona" and the logo "SCM" (which to me has always meant "Student Christian Movement"), the total message consists of the words, "When I was a child, I spake as a child, I understood as a child, I thought as a child: But when I became a man, I put away childish things. *I Corinthians*" (italics in original).

Here indeed is a new model for our annual gift-buying binge: Biblical buttressing. For those who ask, as many surely will, "But what has the *Bible* got to do with Christmas?" we may now be able, thanks to Smith-Corona, to establish some significant connections, hard though it has been to do so in the past. Since Smith-Corona has set the style, we must now ask, "Who follows in their train?" Surely "a cloud of witnesses" (the habit is catching) will gather to expand this new resource for stimulating Christmas sales.

To save the Madison Avenue crowd from having to soil their well-thumbed concordances even further, here are a few suggestions to get the ball rolling (as they say so well down on the Avenue):

• A detailed, even striking, photograph of our most recently perfected missile (brought to use, perhaps, by Lockheed), situated next to the newly projected version of the B-1 bomber, under both of which, after an explanation that nuclear capability is the only way to ensure that our values will be preserved for our children, is a 24-point boldface verity: "Blessed are the peacemakers, for they shall be called sons of God. *Jesus.* " (NOTE to all copy editors: in the spirit of the season, let's keep "Jesus" in italics throughout. Maybe in this one it could even be in *Gothic* italics.)

• An advertisement extolling the virtues of the free-enterprise system, featuring two rising young executives sitting together over martinis, one of them (clearly the "Son" of, say Macfarquar & Son, Realtors) commenting to his friend, "Wist ye not that I must be about my Father's business? *Jesus, as reported by St. Luke as reported by King James.* "

• A color photograph of a Lincoln Continental, or a splendid set of matched golf clubs, undergirded by the caption, "Man shall not live by bread alone."[1]

• A life insurance salesman, sitting in a well-appointed living room, talking to a woman, with a caption to indicate the appropriateness of his being there: "Religion that is pure and undefiled before God and the Father is this: to visit orphans and widows in their affliction. *James.*"

• A sequence sponsored by a health spa, showing how a paunchy middle-aged man can, through a regimen prescribed by said spa, become trim, lithe, and physically attractive once more. Through the sequence can be woven the immortal words of the master body-builder: "I do not run aimlessly, I do not box as one beating the air; but I pommel my body and subdue it. *Paul.*"

• The interior of a substantial-looking bank, featuring an understanding-looking vice-president talking to a worried-looking client with such sincerity as to instill Perfect Confidence. The caption: "Have no anxiety about anything. *Paul.*"[2]

• Gallo Wineries, long under boycott by the United Farm Workers for deficient labor policies, might try a spiritual comeback with the words: "No longer drink only water, but use a little wine for the sake of your

---

[1] In Jewish periodicals, many of which may have an understandable reluctance to upgrade Christmas, the statement can be attributed to "Deuteronomy," a Jewish writer of the post-Exodus period, whereas Christian periodicals can attribute it to "Jesus," who was acquainted with Deuteronomy's writings and borrowed extensively from him. Christians who have difficulty picturing Jesus in a Lincoln Continental, or playing golf with representatives of the principalities and powers, can substitute in their mind's eye one of his followers, perhaps a professional evangelist, doing so. Subliminal connections will do the rest.

[2] The ubiquitous Paul would surely have made it big in the advertising game.

stomach and your frequent ailments. *I Timothy 5.*"

• Should Gallo attempt this, however, the United Farm Workers would be justified in taking space on the adjoining page and superimposing over a picture of their underpaid workers the caption: "The laborer deserves his wages. *I Timothy 5, just a few lines earlier.*"

After all, all's fair in love and the form of war called Christmas advertising.

MOBIL THEOLOGY

WHEN the Mobil Corporation publishes full-page advertisements featuring words like "guilt," "original sin," and "atonement," it is clear that lay theology has finally made it into the big time, and the discipline has been rescued from the professionals. Long has this been my fervent wish; now that the wish has been granted we must examine the results.

Being as hard-nosed as the next guy, I decided to test Mobil's theological assertions through a public opinion survey. The survey was based on a random sampling of 1,249 North Americans evenly divided between males and females (49 percent male, 51 percent female), including 11 percent blacks, and covering a geographical spread guaranteed to preclude skewing of the evidence by sectional interests.

I can report that Mobil has done its work well. It knows where The People are at, and what their deeply felt concerns are. It has found significant ways both to reassure them and, when necessary, to challenge them at a basic level.

The opening line of Mobil's text goes, "Judging by

some of what we read and hear, self-flagellation seems about to become the order of the day." To test the accuracy of this prediction, we posed an initial question to our scientifically selected sample: "What seems to you about to become the order of the day?"

9% replied "atomic warfare."
13.6% replied "professional soccer."
4.9% replied "crime in the streets."
6.1% replied "reruns of 'All in the Family.' "
1.7% replied "close encounters of the fourth kind."
0.7% replied "the three-martini lunch."
64% replied "self-flagellation."

While 64 percent is not an overwhelming majority, it is an impressive one, indicating that Mobil's ear-to-the-grounders have their antennas properly attuned.

In paragraph four, Mobil proposes the following question: "Do you think it's right for the United States, with only 5% of the world's population, to consume 28% of its energy?" Mobil predicts that our answer will be (after beating our breasts), "Heavens to Betsy, no! How could we do such a thing? And how can we atone?"

We discovered that Mobil was even closer to determining the heartbeat of the American people on this one. For when we asked Mobil's identical question to our across-the-board sampling, we found that 69 percent of the population, *over two thirds,* responded with the very phrase predicted by Mobil. The figure is even higher when we include slight verbal variants. Members of the Electrical Workers Union, for example, tended to state their concern with the agonized query, "Geez, what can we do by way of propitiation?" while housepersons in middle to upper income brackets usually engaged in a self-interrogation that went, "How can we align ourselves vicariously with the dispossessed?" It is clear from these responses that 99.44 percent of the American people subscribe to some form of a doctrine of atonement (even if it is mildly Abelardian) and believe that it is as American as Rap Brown and cherry pie. Chalk up another one for Mobil.

Varying our procedure, we used a sampling of Third World peoples to test Mobil's characterization of the United States as ". . . a prime purveyor to the hungry and the needy abroad." We asked: "How would you characterize the United States today in relation to developing nations?" After discounting emotive responses, e.g., those referring to the United States as "imperialist" (43 percent), "dominated by the CIA" (19 percent), and "the pawn of the multinationals" (36 percent), we found that a full 2 percent of the respondents called the United States "a prime purveyor to the hungry and the needy abroad." Here is clear proof indeed that there are those in the Third World who share Mobil's perception of the United States.

Halfway through the ad, Mobil informed us that "we are trying to make two points," the first of which went: "(1) Gratuitous martyrdom is an exercise in futility." Here, interestingly enough, we discern Mobil's willingness to raise a controversial issue and *run counter to the tide.* For when we asked our scientifically selected sample, "What is your opinion of gratuitous martyrdom?" 94 percent responded, "Gratuitous martyrdom is a tested and effective way to get things done. Far from being an exercise in futility, it is the hallmark of the American way of life, the thing above all that has made America great."

It is clear that, on this one, Mobil is wielding a scalpel that must wound before it heals, since the ad *challenges* 94 percent of the American people to forego their deeply felt beliefs and kick their deeply engrained habit of martyring themselves for free.

Mobil challenges yet another cherished conviction: "We cannot believe that Americans can solve or even alleviate the problems of this country and the rest of the world through starvation diets or by sleeping on a bed of nails." While only 61 percent of our sampling felt that we could solve our problems "through starvation diets," *almost 80 percent* (79.69 percent) believed that we could do so "by sleeping on a bed of nails," though allowance must be made for the likelihood that some respondents had been sleeping on a bed of water for a decade and were simply longing for a change. Some affirmed that they were trying to combine the two forms of slumber by sleeping on waterbeds full of *galvanized* nails, in order to lick the rust problem.

A revolutionary theological insight is contained in Mobil's next-to-last paragraph: "To some people pleasure may be a little sinful, but if there were no sin in the world, what would be the benchmark for virtue?" Mobil proposes that we *judge virtue from the perspective of sin,* instead of continuing to do it the old-fashioned way, which was just the reverse. Sin, not virtue, is to be normative.

What fun.

Have the Mobil theologians any idea what they have unleashed? Sin, they have already told us, is self-flagellation; virtue will therefore be the opposite—not flagellation of self but flagellation of others. Sin, they have already told us, is low self-esteem; virtue will therefore be the opposite—not low esteem of self but low esteem of others.

How would the Mobil theologians respond to the familiar Pauline question: "Shall we sin bravely so that virtue may have a benchmark?" They are convicted out of their own mouths: "Heavens to Betsy, no!" they would have to reply. "How could we do such a thing? And how can we atone?"

Full circle.

If this is lay theology, I rest content, particularly when I remember that the top line of the advertisement goes, "Business *and the rational mind,* Part III" (italics added).

Very Mobile.

AUTOMOTIVE THEOLOGY

MY travels in pursuit of saintly deeds shining brightly in a naughty world take me to many places. I recently spent Three Kings Day in France, where I had the cake traditionally associated with the Epiphany season, a cake that is not only flavor-filled but favor-filled as well. One member of our party received a tiny favor in the form of a Christchild, surely an appropriate symbol for the occasion. The other favor, however, turned out to be a racing car. This initially seemed to me like the intrusion of crass secularism into a religious festival, until I reflected that it represented a perfect piece of demythologization in the form of the following Epiphany equation:

$$\frac{\text{camel}}{\text{wise man}} = \frac{\text{racing car}}{\text{modern man}}$$

How would one rush to the manger today? By the most efficient means of ground transportation available. Surely their camel has become our car.

Which leads to a few reflections on the fine art of The Modern Equivalent Of Camel-Driving, i.e., propelling motor vehicles from place to place. I have discovered that certain nations embody certain theological

26

characteristics in their automotive habits.

The whole of the *British* transport system, for example, is incurably papal, and pre-Vatican II papal at that. An irreformable decree was long ago passed, and it is unthinkable on the part of all save pernicious heretics that it should ever be challenged. The decree goes, in rough translation: "The left side is the right side." No matter that progress has long since left this teaching behind or that modern civilization has discarded it. It would be anathema for those who maintained the papal position "to reconcile themselves to progress and modern civilization" (Pius IX, *Syllabus of Errors*).

The influence of Ignatius Loyola is strong here also, and in the *Spiritual Exercises* of every member of the Ministry of Transport is a repetition of his fundamental truth: "If Mother Church so teach me, I will believe left to be right, whatever my senses may suggest." And as we all know, when the papacy and the Jesuits make common cause (an increasingly infrequent occurrence), conformity to their collective will is the surest course for human survival in this world and the next, as all who have driven in Britain can testify.

Britain, it is clear, will yet vindicate her retention of the title given by the pope to Henry VIII before his defection to the Protestant heresy, *Defensor Fidei* (Defender of the Faith).

Sweden, on the other hand, recently displayed her True Protestant temperament by a major piece of *aggiornamento,* reforming the previously irreformable decree so that now (in an instance of the exercise of the "modernist heresy" the true Briton can only deplore) it is not only custom but law that in Sweden the left side is no longer the right side but the wrong side while the right side which was once the wrong side is no longer the wrong side but is now the right side—as transparent an example of Paul Tillich's "Protestant principle" as one could hope to find.

American drivers, of course, are firmly committed Semi-Pelagians, believing that while they operate within some kind of preordained framework (almost Leibnizian in scope), they must contribute mightily to their own salvation. Their contribution consists of such things as (a) staying roughly within certain established speed limits, (b) not transgressing too egregiously against parking regulations, and (c) in general affirming a quasi salvation by works in which a happy issue out of their freeway afflictions is assured only if maximal human effort is continuously expended. Thus faith and works are joined pragmatically, and William James begins to vie with Pelagius for veneration in their worship.

If the above comments seem too generous to the instincts of self-preservation and moderate courtesy among American drivers, they need only be set in the context of experience on *French* highways to assume the character of luminous and self-evident truth. For it is the French theology of driving that is most deeply embedded in the national self-consciousness. All French drivers, *sans exception,* are incurably Augustinian, believing in both original sin and predestination. Not only do they believe in them with an intellectual assent of the will, but they act on the basis of these convictions with unrelenting consistency.

The doctrine of *original sin* on the French highways can be translated: "If you don't get there first, somebody else will." (A variant translation, found in certain manuscripts, goes: "If you give an inch, somebody else will take a mile.") And there is massive empirical evidence to show (a) that nobody else ever gets there first except you, and that if you didn't, you never will; and (b) that a smashed-up car is a small price to pay for having claimed one's inch.

Since every driver operates on these premises, we observe a demythologized way of underlining the further Augustinian truth that original sin has infected the entire race. (The words *massa damnata* are never far from the lips of a French driver.) And if we adopt the modern Freudian notion that automobiles are sex symbols, we can even retain the great African doctor's notion that sin is transmitted through the act of sexual procreation.

But if sin is so pervasive that man[1] has been driven [sic] out of the Garden and onto the stormy highway of life, how is it that man can live by hope? Here is where *predestination and providence* come in, and these comforting doctrines are demythologized in the following manner: "Although it is mathematically impossible for me to get past the car ahead of me before the oncoming truck crashes into me, perhaps I will . . ." So the issue is joined, the accelerator is pressed to the floorboard, and the whole episode is offered up on the altar of belief in providence, nay, special providence.

French drivers thus identify with the Pauline question, "Shall we sin bravely that grace may abound?" although they reject the Pauline response, "God forbid!" To them, God does not forbid but commands, and so they make their own the famous prayer of Augustine that so infuriated Pelagius: "Give what Thou commandest, and command what Thou wilt." And in a surprising number of cases, He[2] does. Q.E.D., as the French are fond of saying.

At one point, however, French drivers have gone modern in a way that has important international consequences. For they combine their traditional Augustini-

---

[1] The sexist language is that of Augustine, not Hereticus. [Ed.]
[2] See footnote 1.

anism ("Love God, and do as you please on the high-way") with "situation ethics," i.e., they have an ethic without rules, save one. Just as situation ethicists affirm one rule, namely, a priority to love, so French drivers affirm one rule, namely, "Priority to the right." At every intersection, this one rule invokes a higher loyalty than such lesser matters of the law as obeying traffic lights, worrying about pedestrian safety, and tithing mint, anise, and cummin.

And it is when we juxtapose the French irreformable decree ("Priority to the right") with the ultramontane allegiance of the British theological school ("The right side is the wrong side") that we understand why an all-wise and all-loving Providence decreed that between two nations with such diametrically opposed commitments there should exist a body of water on top of which the weight of no motor vehicle could ever be sustained.

As for the Italians . . .

THEOLOGICAL STREAKING[1]

STREAKING has not only hit the college campuses; even the hard hats—traditional enemies of the students—have taken it up. Streaking can be defined as "getting down to bare facts" or "stripping away the nonessentials." The true meaning of streaking, of course, is (like all things) theological: streaking is the attempt by a sinful generation to reclaim the lost innocence of the idyllic

---

[1]Readers who feel that articles about "streaking" are *passé* should contain their anxiety until the next-to-last paragraph, where Hereticus' "luminous prescience," referred to in the Preface, is exemplified. [Ed.]

paradise that was the Garden of Eden, before the fall came along and made clothing a tragic necessity.

Theologians frequently engage in their own peculiar brand of streaking, though they tend (after the manner of most theologians) to do it symbolically rather than literally. Only people as pure in heart as St. Francis can engage in streaking that is both symbolic and literal. St. Francis, it will be remembered, when confronted by the stern word of the gospel to forsake all possessions, promptly went to the public square in Assisi and did just that, divesting himself of every bit of clothing, retaining neither tennis shoes nor face mask. The episode points up a crucial difference between saints and theologians: saints take the message literally, theologians take it symbolically. We can be pretty sure it never occurred to St. Francis to demythologize the command.

This is not a plea for theologians to become saints and engage in literal streaking, since I am enough of a realist to know that theologians, whatever else they may be, are never pure in heart. But I do think that streaking ("one of the signs of the times," as Vatican II might have called it) can remind us of the kind of symbolic streaking that theologians exercise as they try, in their own fashion and in ways appropriate to their own discipline, to strip away nonessentials.

The ontological argument is a case in point. Anselm of Canterbury dressed it up in extraordinary verbal finery long before it ever occurred to the theological streakers to get to work on it. The argument runs *in part:*

> Even the fool must be convinced that a being than which none greater can be nor be conceived exists at least in his understanding, since when he hears this he understands it, and whatever is understood is in the understanding. But clearly that than which a greater cannot be nor be conceived cannot exist in the understanding alone. For if

31

it is actually in the understanding alone, it can be thought of as existing also in reality, and this is greater. Therefore, if that than which a greater cannot be nor be conceived is in the understanding alone, this same thing than which a greater cannot be nor be conceived is that than which a greater can be or be conceived. But obviously this is impossible. Without doubt, therefore, there exists, both in the understanding and in reality, something than which a greater cannot be nor be conceived.

That, it must be conceded, is a well-dressed, if not over-dressed, bit of prose. And it took almost nine centuries before that theological-philosophical streaker *par excellence*, Lord Bertrand Russell, succeeded in stripping away all the nonessentials and giving us the ontological argument in its barest form. The argument runs *in full:*

| Being is. |

Lord Russell had to engineer this stripping away virtually bare-handed, since not many of his theological or philosophical predecessors had given him much previous help in the simplification process.

But there are other instances in which a more gradually achieved reduction took place. This time it is the Decalogue that is the case in point. We start out with ten commandments. And while the *Reader's Digest* never got around to reducing the Ten Commandments to perhaps "the four most popular Commandments," we do discover that even by New Testament times the ten have been reduced to two and that the second is said to be like the first. And then, only shortly after the events described in the Gospels, Paul comes along and claims that "the whole law is fulfilled in one word, 'You shall love your neighbor as yourself' " (Gal. 5:14)—a greater instance of Paul's streaking ability than of his mathematical accuracy. Augustine continues the reduction process even further by revising the commandment to read, "Love God, and do as you please," sometimes reported (in an even more telling streaker formula) as "Love, and do as you please." Today both orthodox and liberal streakers carry the process still farther, reducing the command either to "Love God" (the orthodox version) or to "Do as you please" (the liberal version).

The Puritan tradition has been another arena for subsequent theological streaking, since few people have ever written longer treatises than the Puritan divines. When we ask, therefore, "What is a Puritan?" our answer is likely to take pages if not volumes, as we involve ourselves in intricate descriptive accounts of guilt, justification, infralapsarianism, premillennialism, supralapsarianism, and postmillennialism, followed by treatments of a stern and taxing deity making impossible demands even on those of his children whom he chooses not to damn eternally.[2]

How grateful we latter-day sinners can be, therefore, to that iconoclastic streaker, the late H. L. Mencken, who chose to strip away the verbiage and get down to essentials, defining a Puritan as one obsessed with "the haunting fear that somewhere, somehow, someone might be happy."

Where will it all end? Will streaking, both literal and symbolic, continue until all has been permanently reduced to its bare essentials?

I have a theory that applies to both literal and symbolic streaking. Before long (perhaps even before this has appeared in print), the fad will fade. The ongoing human craving for mystery will reassert itself. A new generation will rise up, fascinated on the one hand by the designing and wearing of clothes, and engaged on the other

---

[2]Here is a place where sexist language seems unobjectionable. [Ed.]

hand in the designing and wearing of elaborate theological speculation. It may not be long before we find people praying to a God than whom no greater can be nor be conceived, engaging in new and elaborate midrashic elaborations of the love commandment, and writing, Bunyan-style, their own lengthy twentieth-century equivalents of *Grace Abounding to the Chief of Sinners.*

For if we cannot bear too much reality, we cannot bare it too much either.

EXCLUSIVITY REDIVIVUS; OR, ASSURING IMMORTALITY TO DAVID TRACY

When you own *Wyeth at Kuerners,* you own a copy of the first and only edition. Houghton Mifflin wishes to announce that there will never be another printing. As with our promise on the 1968 edition of *The Work of Andrew Wyeth,* we have destroyed all the plates of *Wyeth at Kuerners.* This means that it, too, will become a collector's item . . . $60.

—Advertisement

. . . Not a new gimmick, of course, but one that the churches used to employ and that the theologians might seek to revive. The principle is clear: Exclusivity. If you have something really beautiful, like a work of art or a gospel of salvation, make sure that only a few people can enjoy it. Guarantee that The Others will never be able to muscle in on the territory, because (as the publishers put it) "We have destroyed all the plates," or (as the church used to put it) "Our offer of salvation is once-for-all. It will never be repeated."

Both promises appear trustworthy. Houghton Mifflin assures us that in A.D. 1968 they destroyed the plates of another book, and theologians have assured us since at least A.D. 68 that the damned outnumber the saved. Earlier predestinarians and latter-day fundamentalists keep the principle alive: a few will make it to salvation, but most won't. You may be one of the lucky few who can have an exclusive privilege that is denied to most.

To be sure, a lot of that ecclesiastical assurance has gone out of style. But Houghton Mifflin is now offering a demythologized version of the same thing: a privilege reserved for the blessed few (in this case purchasable for a mere $60), a modest but attainable form of exclusivity.

But are these promises of bliss-through-exclusivity still trustworthy? Can we *count* on them? St. Karl of Basel once apostrophized: "Peculiar Christendom, whose greatest fear seems to be that one day it might turn out that hell had been depopulated!" Here is as direct a challenge to exclusivity as one could imagine. What if someday a group of similarly motivated publishers got control of Houghton Mifflin and printed a *second edition*, thereby making the book available to all, and not just to the few? Their version of a demythologized *apocatastasis* would go: "Peculiar bookbuyers, whose greatest fear seems to be that one day it might turn out that there was a second edition of *Wyeth at Kuerners!*"

A sobering thought, which has important implications for the publication of theological treatises. The problem in religious book publishing these days is clear: lack of sales. All of us have received rejection slips containing the supreme downer, "It's a great work, but there just isn't a sufficient market to justify publication."

Houghton Mifflin, however, has invoked a useful principle that religious publishers might well emulate: *Instead of seeking to expand sales, limit sales.* Exalt scarcity.

A rejuvenating thought.

Consider the consequences of Seabury Press, say, advertising: "Only ten copies of David Tracy's *Blessed Rage for Order* will be printed. When this initial run is finished, we will destroy the plates forever." The bookstore lines for Fr. Tracy's book would be stupendous. To have *seen* a copy would be a status symbol in itself, to have *read* it would guarantee employment in the Religion Departments of all but land-grant institutions, while to *own* it (valuable collector's item that it would be) would ensure a favorable credit rating toward bank loans beyond comparison.

One could even dismember one's copy, selling single pages at many times the original cost. The fortunes of the market being what they are, a single intact chapter would be worth a king's ransom. Footnotes to chapters could be displayed in rare book rooms of theological libraries and used as bibliographies for advanced seminars, the originals (long since preserved in plexiglass) being made available for personal examination only "with the permission of the instructor." With the passage of time, fragments of the margins, even if containing no printed matter, could (if properly attested) be enclosed in the cornerstones of new church buildings, or, even more appropriately, embedded within altars. We would soon begin to hear of miraculous healings wrought by the mere presence of the relics of *Blessed Rage for Order.*

A further by-product would be that interest engendered by a limited edition might push the fortunate owners to *read the text itself.* In this way the message of the author could be passed on from generation to generation (*in secula seculorum,* as Fr. Tracy himself might have put it in his pre-revisionist days).

There would, of course, be the problem of imitations. Xerox copies could be easily detected and properly scorned, and owners of photocopies, even if almost indistinguishable from the original, could be prosecuted for violating copyright laws. Assuming that Seabury used superior stock for its limited edition (perhaps paper with the same rag content as that on which dollar bills are printed), it would be possible in case of legal disputes to distinguish the originals from the copies by carbon-14 tests or other detection devices known to lovers of incunabula.

I've always intended to read the book myself, but at the present going rate of $12.95 it hardly seems worth the effort. If the price were ten times that, however, or even ten times ten times that, and there were only ten copies in print, I might even mortgage a monastery or two in order to get full control of the market. Then I could either raise the price or (in the interests of heresy) keep everybody else from ever reading the book at all. I'll bet Houghton Mifflin and Seabury never thought of that.

Things Churchy

*(Much of It Devoted to Episcopalians,
Who Are Always Fair Game)*

FIVE WAYS TO UNDERMINE THE PASTOR:
A REAL-LIFE STORY

I DISAGREE

With Practically Everything

to Which

GANSE LITTLE

SUBSCRIBES

—*Abe Hay*

THIS paid advertisement appeared in the *Pasadena Star-News* just before Election Day. It was the disgruntled voice of a member of the Pasadena Presbyterian Church objecting to what his minister was preaching. Once we recover from the moral crudity of the statement (and who are we to boggle at a crudity or two for the sake of morals?), all sorts of charming possibilities present themselves. Here, ready to hand, is a splendid device for destroying Christian community. Nobody exposed to a daily or weekly diet of this sort is likely to be reminded of the bothersome phrase: "See how these Christians love one another!"

Here, consider, is one of those rare situations in American Protestantism in which a minister, rather than merely reflecting the middle-class *mores* of his middle-class congregation, had been speaking a prophetic word. (Dr. Little's chief sin, at the time the advertisement appeared, was his opposition to racial discrimination in housing.) In doing so, he was of course breaking the cardinal rule of successful pulpiteering, "Speak to us smooth things" (Isa. 30:10), which being rendered in the vernacular means: "Don't rock the boat."

In the Good Old Days, those prophets who broke this rule were (a) thrown into cisterns, (b) drawn and quartered, (c) handed over to the Inquisition, (d) excommunicated, (e) fired, or (f) made the object of gossip campaigns.

Today people who squirm under the prophetic thrust have a new technique at their disposal, the mass media. And the modern cry is: Advertise! The mind fairly boggles at the possibilities thus opened up. Here, for use in all situations where applicable, are five possibilities:

1. The Positive-Thinking Approach (in Contrast to Mr. Hay's Sheer Negativism)

I Subscribe

To Practically Everything

with Which

Ganse Little

Disagrees

—Norma Peel

2. The Itemized Documentary Approach

I Disagreed with

GANSE LITTLE'S

Fourth Point

Last Sunday Morning

—Jeanne Burch,
Moral American
Mothers Association

This gets Ms. Burch off the kind of hook on which Mr. Hay could easily find himself impaled (does Mr. Hay reject belief in the Incarnation, the Authority of Scripture, the Communion of Saints, and other things in which we may presume that a Presbyterian pastor believes?). But the Itemized Documentary Approach could backfire. People might want to find out what was in that mysterious fourth point and phone the church for mimeographed copies of the sermon. Worse still, they might read it.

3. The Teen-Age Rebuttal to the Adult Disclaimer

We Dig

GANSE LITTLE

(signed) *Frieda McCauley, Jeff Shorter, Mabel Bockerhausen, Muriel Lemming, Wanda Phelps, Ace Carter, and all the Gang*

4. *The Pious Insinuation*

My Fellow Christians: In spite of what he said last Sunday morning, it would be unfair to draw the conclusion that *Ganse Little is a conscious agent of the Communist Party.* In the name of Christian charity we must refrain from implying that Dr. Little's left-wing views are *directly inspired by the reading of Communist literature,* even though anyone who has been in his study will know that there is a copy of *Das Kapital* displayed prominently (right next to *The Wealth of Nations*). We must remember that while many ministers have imbibed deeply of the Social Gospel and are thus Socialists in their outlook, this does not mean that they give *secret allegiance to communism.* So let us remember that there is no evidence to prove conclusively that *Ganse Little is a Communist.*

In the Name of Our Lord and Savior,

HUNTINGTON H. HUNTINGTON III

5. *Extension of Critique of Minister to Other Aspects of Church Life*

WE BOTH DISLIKED

LAST SUNDAY'S ANTHEM

—*Mr. and Mrs. B. Flatte*

41

Why Does Our Church Use
Grape Juice
When the Episcopalians Use
Wine?
Even Jesus Used Wine (See John 2:1–10)
—*Julio Gallow*

The Superintendent of the Primary
Department
Picks on My Child
Why Can't We Have a Happy Church School?
—*A Disgruntled Father*

If We Continue to Let the Young People Dance
in the Church House, One Thing Will
Lead to Another . . .
—*Methuselah Circle*

People used to look in the Saturday paper to find out what the sermon topic would be. Now they can turn to the Monday edition to discover which church has the best display of soiled ecclesiastical laundry.

GETTING AT THE PASTOR
THROUGH THE PASTOR'S
SPOUSE[1]

"Clergy ought to be celibate because no decent right-minded man ought to have the effrontery to ask any woman to take on such a lousy job. It is thoroughly unchristian."
    —*Ms. Michael Wolfe, wife of an Anglican divine, as reported in the press*

FOR a long time I have been helping my readers discover ways to undermine their pastors.[2] But in so doing I have neglected all the subtle ways in which to instill a sense of vague unease in the men who occupy our pulpits. Now, thanks to Ms. Wolfe, a new avenue of exploitation is open to us: work through the pastor's wife. *Cherchez la femme.*

As Hubert Humphrey was fond of remarking, behind every successful man stands a surprised mother-in-law. I suggest that behind every pastor stands a disgruntled

---

[1]Here we have one of the most delicate problems of the *Zeitgebund* nature of some of Hereticus' early pieces. The terms of the critique launched by Ms. Wolfe clearly imply that "clergy" is an exclusively masculine term. This is no longer true even in the denomination to which she belongs. But since that denomination is successfully keeping most of its ordained women from becoming parish priests, the polemic still has virtually universal applicability. An interesting exercise for readers sensitive to the sexist issue, however, will be to reverse the sexual attribution each time it appears, e.g., "she" for "he," "he" for "she," and so on. One can then determine how much progress has been made. [Ed.]

[2]The author is obviously referring to a series in his previous volume, *The Collect'd Writings of St. Hereticus,* entitled "Undoing the Pastor's Work." [Ed.]

spouse. At least, if she is not already disgruntled, it is our job to make her so. For once the seeds of domestic discord have been planted, while some may fall on stony ground, others will grow and flourish, some thirty, some sixty, some an hundredfold.

A few sample gambits:

1. *The Prayer Meeting Plot.* This is a subtle and fiendishly successful device, successful because the one who plants the seed never need water it again, that task being energetically taken on by others. The device is to pray publicly for the minister during the intercessions at a monthly church meeting. My appointed delegate, eyes closed and pious look affixed, storms the gate of heaven with the following: ". . . and in conclusion, O Lord, we ask thy special blessing on our minister in this time of his home difficulty, asking that thou wilt give him patience and understanding and, above all, a forgiving spirit."

There is nothing quite like an announcement of this sort, apparently directed to the Almighty but really crafted for local consumption, to get the tongues wagging. If pressed after the meeting, my helper is instructed to say quietly: "I really mustn't say anything more. You don't think it was indiscreet of me to mention their problem, do you?"

2. *The Damned-If-She-Does-And-Damned-If-She-Doesn't Attack.* The minister's wife either (a) takes an active part in the parish, or (b) does not take an active part in the parish. The attack is very simple: if (a) is true, employ (b) as a norm and criticize her in terms of it. Or vice versa.

First alternative: "It's all very well for the minister's wife to do a lot in the parish, but she doesn't have to act as if she *owns* the place, does she? I mean, after all, there are other people who can play the piano too. And why *she* should be the one to lead the ladies' devotional every week is more than I can understand. You'd think she'd realize that other people know how to work up a nice little worship service too. If she wants to teach a Sunday school class, I suppose that's all right, though with all those children of hers at home you'd think she'd give them a little more time."

Second alternative: "I can't understand why the new minister's wife has to act so superior. You'd think she didn't *care* about the church! She refused to play the piano for the women's meeting yesterday—said she'd done it last week. And when I asked her to lead the devotions she said once a month was enough for anyone, and why didn't I do it myself. Really! If she only knew how long it takes to work up a really sincere little worship service, she wouldn't be quite so quick to dump it in other people's laps. And just because she has four preschool children she thinks she can get out of teaching Sunday school. The last minister's wife was superintendent of the Sunday school from the day she arrived. . . . You'd think this one would have been glad for the chance to serve."[3]

Third alternative: Whenever the minister's wife shows signs of vacillating from a clear-cut policy, she can be accused of playing favorites, e.g., "She wouldn't organize a rummage sale for *me,* even though I asked her three times, but the minute Mrs. Benson asked her to serve punch she absolutely jumped at the chance."

---

[3]A special effect can be gained by concluding the above peroration with the words ". . . in the Kingdom."

3. The Impact of Innuendo and Illicit Inference. Easier to illustrate than describe:

a. "My dear, I think it's perfectly wonderful the way you don't complain about your husband paying so many pastoral calls on that attractive Miss Simpson who moved here recently. And in the evening, too . . ."

b. "I hope you don't mind my phoning you on your husband's day off. I know he said the two of you were going off somewhere for the day—your wedding anniversary, isn't it?—but my Jimmie is in the fifth grade play at 11:30 this morning, and it would mean *so* much to him if your husband would show up."

c. "Yes, Ralph told me they *did* talk at the vestry meeting about raising your husband's salary, but he's *so spiritual* they knew he would resent it if they seemed to be tempting him with the things of this world. God and mammon, you know. . . . How fortunate you are to have a marriage where spiritual things come first."

I won't guarantee that all of these gambits were tried on Ms. Wolfe, but I'm sure that if I could just sign her up as a guest (or ghost) writer sometime, she could make them sound tame by comparison.

KEEPING UP
WITH THE EPISCOPAL JONESES

SINCE I do not have true-blue Episcopal credentials, I occasionally do a little reverse slumming by glancing at the literature prepared for those who do. A splendid opportunity was recently afforded by the Lenten-Spring catalog of an Anglican supply house.

The first thing to notice about Episcopal spring fashions is that they have gone ecumenical. Those who feared that the "bridge church" might find itself cut off at both ends can relax. As early as page 3 we find a blurb for "Lutheran Liturgy Posters. An effective Aid for Understanding Liturgy. Although these posters were originally produced for the Lutherans, we thought the appropriateness of the material was conducive to our own efforts . . ." (Twenty-four posters for only $2.95.) It is hard to see how it could have been more graciously put, and it would surely be possible to use these posters to special effect before Reformation Sunday each fall.

Bargain Rates on Golgotha Hill Department: A sermon by the Archbishop of Canterbury on the theme "Christ Crucified for the World" can now be obtained for Lenten reading (offer expires on April 30) for the low, low price of 23 cents.

Another difficult problem about Anglicanism (viz., where will it turn if a choice is forced between Geneva and Rome?) is made sumptuously clear by the advertisement for clerical collars. The Anglican has one choice only, albeit in three styles. The only clerical collar he can purchase has the un-Anglican and un-Genevan sounding label "Pontiff." Low churchmen can get Pontiff No. 1 (front height 1"), broad churchmen can get Pontiff No. 2 (front height 1 1/4"), while the really high churchmen can go all the way with Pontiff No. 3 (a full 1 1/2" high in front). It costs no more to be a No. 3 than a No. 1 (60¢ on the line, whatever your ecclesiology), a fact that ought to reassure non-Anglicans that sociological factors do not affect Anglican churchmanship.

In their use of St. Christopher, the catalog writers show how ancient traditions can be adapted to new styles and situations. Old-style Christopher medals apparently had a habit of dropping off the dashboards of new-style automobiles, leaving their owners temporarily bereft of the intercessory powers of the saint in question. So Item 191-372, "St. Christopher Auto Set" is "a new self-stick medal, designed especially for the new, padded dashboards"—as handily an illustration of *aggiornamento* as can be imagined ($1.50 provides this uninterrupted intercessory coverage, gift-boxed).

Ambulatory protection from St. Christopher is also available. One can get a St. Christopher Key Chain "of rugged durability" with a medal that has the words "St. Christopher Protect Us" on one side and a plain, unmarked reverse side ($4.95 gift-boxed). Those who want greater protection than this affords can get the ultimate in assurance, a Christopher medal with added back-up protection in case St. Christopher fails to come through; this one has a reverse side that reads, "In case of an emergency please call an Episcopal Priest." Only $2.05 extra.

Sandwiched in among the St. Christopher medals is Item MB-5, "A thick, masculine Latin Cross." No reference is made elsewhere to "feminine crosses," but the possibilities are intriguing, particularly as one faces the likelihood that one day the Episcopal Church will cross the ecclesiastical Rubicon of ordaining women.[1]

Rugged equipment for all occasions, in fact, seems to be the keynote this spring. Laity are invited to purchase an "Episcopal Church Emblem Tile" for their pastor to hang in his office (No. 6022, $15.00). This tile has the advantage that "it will not chip," which should provide solid assurance for the pastor facing a stormy counseling session on marital problems, or the entrance into his

---

[1]It has since done so, but "feminine crosses" are not yet being advertised, perhaps because they are still being carried on the backs of the women priests themselves. [Ed.]

study of an Exxon vice-president dismayed by a slighting pulpit reference to multinational corporations.

Laity can give the pastor's family a set of Apostles' Spoons, available in any number from one to twelve, at a price of $8.00 each. Discerning families can convey a message by their choice of spoons, since each spoon is inscribed with the name of an Apostle. "Peter" could be chosen for the rector who is a true rock, although such a choice might be equivocal, suggesting that the clergy-man had thrice denied his Lord or tried to walk on water. "Matthew" would be appropriate for the clergy-man who has managed to keep the tax collectors at bay or balanced the budget.

But the family who decides to undermine clerical morale by giving spoons depicting a certain apostle whose credentials are open to question will find that the supply house has played a clever trick, for the description of the spoons ends with the words: "NOTE—The Manufacturer has substituted St. Paul for Judas." Not very Biblical, perhaps, but manifestly guaranteed to pro-mote parish harmony.

On the "church in the world" theme there is a nice pair of Florentine Stamp Boxes, "Antique gold embossed with beautifully hand-tooled finish," complete with "two hinges for easy opening," one of which has the "Madonna of the Chair," while the other has the "Madonna of the Streets," both in living color. If recipients run out of stamps and lose their serenity thereby, the manufacturer offers a "Florentine Serenity Prayer Plaque" (No. 870, only $1.20). The Florentine Serenity Prayer Plaque, also in living color, turns out to contain a prayer by that grand old Florentine, Reinhold Niebuhr.

For the ultimate in ecclesiastical identification, how-ever, it is impossible to beat item No. 521, the "Head of Christ Medal" ($2.10). Sure enough, there is a head of

Christ on one side and a comforting verse of Scripture on the other side, attributable surely to Jesus himself—one of the great "I am" passages of the Fourth Gospel. This particular quotation (missing from my version of the Fourth Gospel) is a clear and succinct self-identification: "I am Episcopalian."

ON APOSTOLIC SUCCESS(ION)

LOUISVILLE, KY.—A move to ordain women as priests was defeated today by the Episcopal House of Deputies.
—*News item, October 4, 1973*

A NARRATIVE APPROPRIATE TO THE ABOVE OCCASION, CON-
TAINING A DESCRIPTION OF CERTAIN LAMENTABLE EVENTS,
TOGETHER WITH A PROGNOSTICATION CONCERNING THEIR
OUTCOME, IN WHICH JUST RETRIBUTION IS VISITED UPON
THE MISCREANTS
(With apologies to Henry Wadsworth Longperson)

Listen, my children, and you shall hear
Of a famous Episcopal move to the rear.
'Twas the fourth of October in seventy-three,
Hardly a woman with mind still free
But remembers that famous day and year.

On the morn of that day back in seventy-three,
The Deputies met down in Louisville, Ky.,
Where up-to-date churchpersons wanted to hope
That the women could soon don the mitre and cope
And be part of Episcopal hierarch-y.

But prudence (that medieval virtue renowned)
Suggested that women should not be unbound.
"The time is not ripe," it was argued by some,
"For women to stand in the place of God's Son
And by font and by altar and pulpit be found."

"This blow," it was argued, "would gain women's
  rights
At prohibitive cost to our masculine rites.
There'd be satins at matins, there'd be disarray
When the priest genuflected or knelt down to pray.
Imagine Episcopal versions of tights!"

So listen, my children, the church's decree
May last till the twenty-first century.[1]
With utmost deliberate speed it's been said
That any church change is effectively dead:
No woman shall enter a male sacrist-y.

"There is still," it was argued, "a role left for women;
While they cannot forgive, they can still be forgiven.
While they can't serve communion, they still can serve
  tea,
And work for the church nonepiscopally,
And thus do the will of their Father in heaven."

But the women no longer would take it in stride.
Since Episcopal status once more was denied,
They worked out a plan, every Mrs. and Ms.;
Until church ordination was hers and/or his
They would sponsor a modern Pauline Revere Ride.

---

[1]The fact that this prediction was fulfilled considerably ahead of
Hereticus' timetable in no way invalidates the possibility that the consequences sketched in the final five lines will be true by 1984. The recent
decision of the Church of England to postpone consideration of the
matter for what will de facto be at least a decade lends verisimilitude
to his prediction as far as global Episcopalianism is concerned. [Ed.]

Now listen once more, of the ride you shall hear,
When the Deputies managed to conquer their fear
('Twas early in March in nine-teen eighty-four,
An Orwellian portent one best not ignore)
And their mind-set was finally made lucidly clear.

By a vote of one hundred and sixteen to one
Episcopal sanction the women had won,
To receive ordination, absolve, catechize,
Write pastoral letters, and even baptize.
"An idea whose time," it was argued, "has come!"[2]

*(So great a change requires two extra beats per line to con-
clude:)*

The press and the rest of the church became lyrical,
But the action turned out to be quite nonempirical.
For the membership rolls, when subjected to search,
Showed that women had long since forsaken the
    church
(A midnight departure that's hardly a miracle).

LORD'S PRAYER, PARAPHRASES OF

Lingering Tillichian

Ground of Being,
No object among other objects,
Aaahhh.
        Be

---

[2]Read footnote 1 again, this time very carefully, before proceeding.
[Ed.]

In history as well as beyond history.
Support our finite freedom,
And sustain us when our dreaming innocence
Becomes *Zeitgebund.*
      For with you alone
Are autonomy and heteronomy
Eternally theonomous.

Pentagon

O Thou Great Chief of Staff,
Supreme in the Chain of Command,
Keep us on top.
We fight for you, we kill for you,
From bombers (as it were) in heaven.
Give us a budget
Commensurate with our needs.
And forgive us our overkill
As we forgive the Chilean *Junta.*
Lead us not into land wars,
And deliver us from Senate hearings.
For if Yours is the Kingdom
Ours is the (air) power
And also the glory.
Unless Russia drops one first.
At ease.

Catholic Left

Father of Dan and Phil and Sister Liz,
You're where it's at.
Your name is justice.
Confound the courts, release the captives,
Right now and not next week.
      Bread and wine
      Will do us fine.
Grant amnesty to prisoners

Just as we hope we would to politicians.
Make The Establishment unattractive,
And keep it that way,
So we look only to you
From Catonsville to Armageddon.

Catholic Right

Pater noster, qui es in caelis;
Sanctificetur nomen tuum;
Adveniat regnum tuum;
Fiat voluntas tua, sicut in caelo, et in terra.
Panem nostrum quotidianum da nobis hodie;
Et dimitte nobis debita nostra,
Sicut et nos dimittimus debitoribus nostris.
Et ne nos inducas in tentationem.
Sed libera nos a malo.
Amen.

Feminist

Beloved Mother,
Not only other
But near,
Your Queendom come,
Your cause be won
Right here.
Give equal rights to us this day,
Forgive the men for what they say
And do.
Destroy exploitation
And male domination,
And save us from chauvinists
Who
Deny that the Queendom
And all that goes with it's for
You.

REVISIONS
FOR
*THE OXFORD DICTIONARY
OF THE CHRISTIAN CHURCH*

(Reflections after spending six hours on an airplane with nothing worth reading but same, and finally discovering a couple of typos)

alienation—a typographical elision, recently adopted by Third World theologians to describe principalities and powers that threaten them (cf. the pastoral letter of the Bolivian archbishop of Titicaca: "Peru is an alienation").

antithesis—a misprint of a term drawn from the writings of Hegel, G. W. F. (q.v.). The actual term, in Hegel's earliest writings, was *antitheos,* a combination of Latin and Greek words meaning, roughly, "against God" (or as it began to appear in the writings of Cerveza, a second-century theological opponent of Lactantius "contra Deum"). A pious typesetter, I. Vino Veritas, upset by the implications of the concept of *antitheos* for the masses (who were eagerly devouring Hegel's early writings) cleverly substituted an "si" for an "o," thus transforming *theos* into *thesis,* a mistake Ph.D. candidates have been making ever since.

Buber, Martin. See *Bucer, Martin.*

"dearth of God" theology—a movement popular in the American churches that lasted about 45 minutes one hot July morning in 1976, when 12,641 worship services

55

were held in the United States featuring pledges of allegiance, waving of flags, singing of the ethnic anthem ("José, can you see?"), countless references to Valley Forge, Ticonderoga, the Emancipation Proclamation, Exxon, the gold standard, and Senator Goldwater, but a dearth (see above) of references to the God of the Bible.

ecclesia—from the Greek, meaning literally "called out," taken over for theological usage from the secular realm (as have been so many other theological terms), in this case from the North American cultural experience of baseball, as in "He was *ecclesia* (or "called out") at home."

Hepatitis—a common heresy (q.v.) induced by looking at the world with a jaundiced complexion.

EPISCOPATE—acronym for the movement of Evangelical Pastors Inducing Schismatic Concern Over Priestly And Theological Excesses. Headquarters in Muncie, Indiana, but often at sea flying the Liberian flag, in order to embody a global perspective and receive certain tax benefits.

Hegel, G. W. F.—German philospher of the nineteenth century, remembered chiefly as the victim of a typesetter's prank.

heresy—mispelling of "hearsay," i.e., a position arrived at on less than total evidence, but infinitely more interesting as a result.

't Hooft, W. A. Visser—frequently cited as editor of many ecumenical publications, but in reality the creation of an ingenious linotype operator in Geneva, who wanted to drive card catalog filers frantic with the unresolved question, "Does he go under 't' or 'H'?" First cousin of Etaoin Shrdlu, the great Amsterdam liturgist.

"Kierkegaard"—a pseudonym employed by the nineteenth-century Danish philosopher Johannes Climacus (1813–1855). Climacus, a native of the Jutland heath, could

not gain acceptance in Copenhagen high society, so, employing a clever ruse, he wrote under the name of "Kierkegaard" (literally "church guard," or "guardian of the church," and thus, by inference, "defender of establishment orthodoxy"). In the 1940's Walter Lowrie started a rumor that "Climacus" was really Kierkegaard, which is not the same thing at all, even though it was good for sales at Princeton University Press.

revelation. See *revolution.*

revolution. See *revelation.*

't Hooft, W. A. Visser—frequently cited as editor of many ecumenical publications, but in reality the creation of an ingenious linotype operator in Geneva, who wanted to drive card catalog filers frantic with the *still* unresolved question, "Does he go under 't' or 'H'?" First cousin of Etaoin Shrdlu, the great Amsterdam liturgist.

FIGURE 47. *Wienowski being ordained through a loophole in canon law.*

Wienowski, Stanislaus (1864–1891)—a Ukrainian Pole from Transylvania, member of the "Old Catholic" Church (q.v.), whose allegiance to Orthodoxy (q.v.) was unquestioned. Ordained at the age of 7, through a loophole in canon law (see Figure 47), Fr. Wienowski completed a dissertation on "Transubstantiation in Transylvania," for which he was subsequently martyred, since his assigned topic had been "Consubstantiation in Carpathia." He was posthumously known as Blessed Stanislaus (cf. further Robert T. Handy's perceptive volume *A Perceptive Retrospective: Memories of a Middle-European Upbringing*, Vandenhoeck & Ruprecht, 1921, xxiii + 7 pp., fully indexed).

Ecumania

MULTIPLE-CHOICE OPTIONS:
(COUNCIL-, GENERAL ASSEMBLY-,
GENERAL CONVENTION-) -MANSHIP

BY the late 1970's, most of the devices for exploiting ecclesiastical events (Vatican Councils, papal elections, etc.) have been worn thin. But other ecclesiastical meetings continue to take place—Synods of Bishops, General Conventions, General Assemblies, annual meetings, synodical councils, consistories, and the like. They all need interpretation despite the fact (or more accurately, because of the fact) that those On The In want to keep strict control of interpreting what actually went on.

How to meet this situation? How to provide a significant overview of What Really Happened? How to appear knowledgeable in spite of ignorance? How to give the impression of having smashed the Secrecy Curtain that surrounds most ecclesiastical gatherings even though unsure of its actual location?

Having thought deeply about these matters, I have come up with a formula, derived initially from observing the Second Vatican Council, that is nevertheless applicable to all ecclesiastical gatherings and most individual ecclesiastical happenings. Lapidary in form, it goes as follows: *Maneuver the opponent into making a judgment about the gathering, and then disagree with the judgment no matter what it is.*

So much for the principle. Now to some examples. (NOTE: in the models that follow, choose the word in parentheses most appropriate to the situation under discussion.)

1. *The real meaning of Catholic teaching on (collegiality, birth control, ordination of women).* Opponent: "Properly understood, *(De Ecclesia, Humanae Vitae, the Report of the Papal Commission)* opens up vast new realms for a fresh understanding of (collegiality, birth control, the ordination of women)." Counterthesis: "On the contrary, as the text itself makes painfully clear, and as the Pope (himself, himself, himself) has declared, nothing at all has been changed in Catholic teaching about (collegiality, birth control, the ordination of women). How unfortunate that the conservatives really won the victory there."

(NOTE: Observe that these are Classic Articulations of the two positions. This is indicated by the crucial words of each argument; in the first, "Properly understood, . . ." implying that there are infinite exegetical possibilities for those who are not bound by clod-like literalism; and in the second, " . . . as the text itself makes painfully clear," calling a halt to flights of subjective fancy and insisting on a no-nonsense approach consistent with the most rigorous and widely accepted hermeneutical principles.)

Contrariwise, when Opponent insists that *(De Ecclesia, Humanae Vitae, the Report of the Papal Commission)* changes nothing, the counterthesis goes: "But surely that is a superficial interpretation. Naturally the Catholic Church is not going to engage in any publicly announced 'changes.' But the implications of *(De Ecclesia, Humanae Vitae, the Report of the Papal Commission)* open up undreamed-of possibilities for both doctrinal and structural development, maturing (as Newman said so well) when the time is ripe. I predict that within fifty years the whole structure of the church will have changed as a result." (NOTE: Prediction-making should pick a *terminus ad quem* beyond the anticipated life-span of either disputant, or, at the least, that of the Opponent.)

2. *The real meaning of Protestant teaching on (God, church, salvation, eschatology).*
For everyone: "How did (Van Buren, Kaufman, Marty, Robinson, Gilkey, Cox, H. Jackson Forstman) put it in his latest article?"

3. *Assessment of church leaders.* Opponent: "The (pope, moderator, bishop) is basically a conservative at heart." Counterthesis: "On the contrary, the (pope, moderator, bishop) is a remarkably astute progressive who sees the need to make haste slowly and to move in such a way that (he, he, he) can draw all elements in the church along with (him, him, him). This is the only viable route to truly radical change."
Contrariwise, when Opponent insists that the (pope, moderator, bishop) is a progressive, the counterthesis goes: "How, then, do you explain the disappointing character of (his, his, his) long-promised reforms and the discouraging nature of (his, his, his) pronouncements on women's ordination, for example, when seen against the initial hopes that (his, his, his) constituency had had for (him, him, him)?"

4. *Assessing public assessments of ecclesiastical gatherings.* An example drawn directly from Vatican II can make the point with a specificity impossible to generalized statements. Opponent: "Xavier Rynne's treatments of

the Council were the most illuminating." Counterthesis: "For journalistic impressions, I suppose, Rynne is as good as anything in that genre, but the two 'must' treatments of the Council are surely Laurentin's *Bilan de la Deuxième session,* and, *of course,* Häring's *Das Konzil im Zeichen der Einheit.* " (NOTE: Reiterated use of the words "of course" in such discussion renders rejoinder almost impossible.)

Contrariwise, when Opponent commends Laurentin and Häring, the counterthesis goes: "For specialized treatment of certain aspects of the Council, the continental writers are, *of course,* useful. But when all is said and done, no writer has even approached the comprehensiveness of Rynne's four volumes. How tiresome to have a work depreciated as unscholarly just because the writer happens to write robust English prose." (NOTE: Reiterated use of the words "of course" does not always render rejoinder impossible. One may occasionally be hoist on his or her own petard.)

5. *The church's attitude toward (disarmament, revelation, monopoly capitalism).* Opponent: "The decision by the (pope, moderator, bishop) to take this matter out of the hands of the (council, general assembly, general convention) indicates quite clearly that (he, he, he) is afraid to have full and free discussion of so delicate an issue." Counterthesis: "On the contrary, the (pope, moderator, bishop) realized that at this time in history the (council, general assembly, general convention) would collectively be very conservative and one-sided on the matter. Thus it was precisely to ensure what you call a full and free discussion that the (pope, moderator, bishop) turned the matter over to a special commission of (his, his, his) own choosing."

Contrariwise, when Opponent suggests that it was

astute to take the matter out of the hands of the (council, general assembly, general convention), the counterthesis goes: "But the only way, in an age of (councils, general assemblies, general conventions), to have a significant breakthrough is for the (council, general assembly, general convention) to deal with the matter itself. A (papal, moderatorial, episcopal) commission is just that—a *(papal, moderatorial, episcopal)* commission—and represents a bypassing of the importance of the (council, general assembly, general convention), not to mention (the apostolate of the laity, the priesthood of all believers, the house of deputies)."

On most matters where interpretative estimates are called for, the full evidence will be unavailable for decades, by which time most of the discussants will be safe in Abraham's bosom, where such matters can be viewed from a perspective of more generous amplitude. Should it be the case, however, that one's short-range reaction turns out to be wrong, such intellectual misadventure can be passed off by indicating that inside sources were themselves erratic and unreliable, viz: "Thank heavens the (curia, presbytery, bishops, moderators) were finally persuaded to change their tactics. The talk in (Rome, Geneva, Canterbury, Grand Rapids) only a few weeks ago was that they had determined to make a last-ditch stand. It is a source of great satisfaction to learn that cooler heads prevailed."

With a little practice, such techniques can be adapted to all other questions, viz., the future of Teilhard de Chardin in Catholic theology, the state of the seminaries, the subject of Martin Marty's forthcoming book, the content of Karl Rahner's last book, the future of Polish papal jokes, and (our gravest problem) the proper pronunciation of "ecumenism."[1]

OUR GRAVEST PROBLEM:
THE PROPER PRONUNCIATION
OF "ECUMENISM"

IT is important to remember that if all other barriers fall, one final stumbling block will remain. Until it has been resolved, other matters of ecumenical discussion are so much peripheral trivia. I refer, of course, to the key problem: how to pronounce "ecumenism."

The situation surrounding this problem is one that John Leo has described, with reticence, as "total chaos." Even Karl Rahner's investigations, thus far available only in German, have failed to clarify matters. To be blunt: Those who cannot pronounce what they espouse are unlikely to command the respect of those whose commitment they seek to enlist—a sentiment surely worthy of being carved in marble.

Since the word has four syllables, we confront four possibilities of pronunciation:

1. In good Biblical fashion we can let the last be first and start with ec-u-men-*ism*. The only advantage of this pronunciation is that so far nobody has used it, and thus nobody has a vested interest in it. Its adoption would therefore ensure that no ecumenical participant could claim a victory. (The possible exception would be the *periti* of Vatican II who, after four years of experience in such matters, would soon determine that such a pronunciation is indeed what the church has always taught, "having been the preferred pronunciation of St. Peter and the unfailing choice of all his successors, of happy memory, in that ancient and venerable see.")

The disadvantage, however, outweighs any possible

---

¹See next essay. [Ed.]

advantage, namely, that "-isms" are suspect. "Secularization" may be in, but "secularism" is out. So are "fascism," "totalitarianism" and "caesaropapism." Ec-u-men-*ism* is tarred by the same brush.

2. Turning from last to first, *ec*-u-men-ism is a live option. Its popularity might have become universal had not an insuperable difficulty recently been raised. For as Quanbeck, Lindbeck, Dietzfelbinger, and Schlink have pointed out in *Dialogue Derailed,* the pronunciation is unacceptable to Lutherans. The reiteration of the word ("*ec*-u-men-ism, *ec*-u-men-ism") sounds like a taunting reminder of the Leipzig Disputation of July 1519 between Martin Luther and Johann Eck ("*Eck*-u-men-ism, *eck*-u-men-ism"), seeming to suggest that Luther did not win the disputation, and that by a clever trick it is his opponent who is to be immortalized.

3. A third alternative is the third syllable, ec-u-*men*-ism. Its advantages are two: (a) like the first alternative, it has not been used before and possesses all the rights and privileges thereto appertaining, and (b) it conforms to the current pronunciation of the adjective ("ec-u-*men*-i-cal"), thus introducing consistency, a virtue not always discernible on the ec-u-*men*-i-cal scene.

The argument would be compelling save for a single and insurmountable objection, voiced by groups as diverse as the Sisters of the Blessed Virgin Mary, the Catholic Mothers Sodality, and the National Association of Protestant Church Women. These groups refuse to countenance any suggestion that ecumenical activity is a male prerogative. I can report flatly: "ec-u-*men*-ism" doesn't stand a chance. Scratch it.

4. This leaves only one alternative, ec-*u*-men-ism. (NOTE: Care must be taken not to render the pronunciation e-*cu*-men-ism since, as a perceptive critic pointed out, this has many unhelpful overtones, viz.: (a)

"Q," which suggests higher criticism, which suggests watering down the faith, (b) "queue," i.e., queuing up for rebaptism, (c) "cue," associated with pool halls and shady deals, and (d) "queue," which suggests a certain type of Eastern hairstyle and implies the inclusion of Oriental religions. The pronunciation must be carefully nuanced. Only such precision in small matters will forestall the possibility of doctrinal indifferentism on higher levels.)

The arguments in favor of ec-*u*-men-ism are two, the first decisive, the second strategic. (a) The decisive argument is that since we have discovered that nothing else will do, this must. As John Courtney Murray would put it, "The argument is unanswerable." (b) Strategically, the pronunciation provides a new slogan (and for the grass roots, a slogan is an ecumenical necessity): "Don't let the other person do all the work. Get with it yourself. Put the 'you' in 'ec*u*menism.' "

EMILY'S POST-COUNCIL BOOK
OF ECUMENICAL ETIQUETTE

DURING the era of Ecumenical Euphoria you made some new friends and you want to know how to keep them even though things have quieted down. The Protestants have long since visited St. Figita's Church and discovered that there is no arsenal in the basement for The Takeover When They Get To Be 51 Percent. The Roman Catholics have long since visited the Lutheran Church of the Redeemer and discovered that the Lutherans are already singing that new Communion hymn written for the English version of the Catholic Mass, called "A Mighty Fortress Is Our God." How today to

66

maintain the warm glow induced by these early experiences?

A few rules for guidance until the definitive text appears:

1. *Never trust earlier rules for ecumenical etiquette.*

PROTESTANTS: You learned only recently that a Catholic bishop is addressed as "Your Excellency." But try that in public now, and, even though you may win the bishop to the cause of ecumenism, every lay Catholic within earshot will cringe. (NOTE: First-naming a bishop, viz., "Hello there, Clyde!" is still considered avant-garde. It may be done in private, but not to His Excellency's face. Scratch the next-to-last word.)

CATHOLICS: You learned only recently to call Protestant ministers "Reverend." But no more. "Reverend" is bad form. "Dr." them to death; they'll love it (particularly if they don't have a doctorate). Or "Mr." them to death (cf. priesthood of all believers); they'll love it, particularly if they have a doctorate (about which they will let you find out later so that you can describe them as "truly humble"). Exception: high-church Anglicans, who don't consider themselves Protestants anyhow, want to be "Father'd." If you're not sure which they are, don't worry; they'll let you know. This can also remind you of Olden Times when you called *your* priest "Father" instead of "Eugene" or "Ted."

2. *Linguistic instructions:*

a. *Latin is out.*

Protestants who finally found out what the *Pater Noster* was have had to bury the knowledge deep in their subconscious, especially if they are bothered by sexist language and feel uncomfortable about rubbing salt in feminist wounds by speaking about "The Our Father." It is still good form, however, for Protestants to stop praying after the words "Deliver us from evil," thus indicating a real concern for Catholic historical sensibilities, and for Catholics to continue, "For thine is the Kingdom . . . ," etc., showing that they grant Protestants the right to monkey around with the dominical text.

b. *But a little Latin is far out.*

Protestants can show a genuine sensibility to some of the linguistic losses that leave all but the most case-hardened Catholics slightly wistful, by larding their ecumenical conversation with such phrases as *mea culpa!* ("I beg your pardon"), *Kyrie eleison!* (really Greek, but most Catholics won't know that; roughly equivalent in the new vernacular to "Give me another chance, *please?*"), *Populorum progressio* ("Development is the new name for peace"). Catholics may be touched if the Protestant says, with a certain tone of satisfaction, about last Sunday's Methodist liturgy, "We've restored the *Nunc Dimittis.*"

3. *Catholics must not use the word "sects."*

It used to be customary Catholic practice to refer to "the Protestant sects." This must now be disavowed, because: (a) the Protestants with whom Catholics are talking will understand the word pejoratively, and pejorative connotations are un-okay in ecumenical etiquette; and (b) the word on Catholic lips is likely to be interpreted as the opening gambit in a conversation about birth control, e.g., "What does your church think about sects?" Slurring references to "the lack of sects' education" must also be avoided.

4. *Nobody nowadays knocks Martin Luther.*

Catholics, especially when they have seen John Osborne's play about Luther's digestive tract, are not to make cute little jokes about "the diet of Worms." These were old hat 200 years ago. Lutherans, on the other hand, are encouraged to say from time to time, in the closest approximation of deprecatory comment now appropriate, "Well, after all, Luther wasn't God." This is most effective on the lips of Lutherans named Jaroslav Pelikan.

5. *Detailed information in a specialized area of the thought of the ecumenical counterpart is effective.*

SUGGESTION TO CATHOLICS: Memorize *all* the details of the most recent structural reorganization of the World Council of Churches and talk about them often.

SUGGESTION TO PROTESTANTS: Read one diocesan paper (from another part of the country) and refer to it in such a way as to leave the impression that you read them all. West Coast Protestants should quote from the *Delmarva Dialogue* (Wilmington, Delaware), while those east of East St. Louis, Illinois, should refer frequently to *The Catholic Voice* (Oakland, California).

SUGGESTION TO BOTH CATHOLICS AND PROTESTANTS: A certain atmosphere can be created by starting a speech at an ecumenical gathering as follows: "In last week's *Sunday Visitor . . .*"

6. *Sympathy for the ecumenical trauma through which the counterpart's church is going may even help the unscrupulous to score points.*

Either:

"Even as a Protestant I can understand the Pope's dilemma in dealing with the question of women's ordination, since to bring about 'change' will seem to compromise the authority of the *magisterium.*" (NOTE: In the light of Rule 2, subsection A, above, scratch the last word and substitute "teaching office," but pronounce the words with an ever-so-slight hesitation, as though mentally making a translation.)

Or:

"It must be terribly hard for you Protestants to get used to the fact that we Catholics have believed in justification by faith, the priesthood of all believers, and the authority of Scripture all along."

ONE-UP(PSALA)MANSHIP
IN 8 (EIGHT) SECTIONS,
WITH NUMEROUS SUBSECTIONS

A WORLD ASSEMBLY of the World Council of Churches was held in Uppsala, Sweden, in July 1968. Another was held in Nairobi, Kenya, in November-December 1975, and yet another will be held in Vancouver, Canada, so the rumors attest, sometime in the early 1980's. In relation to any such gathering, we discover that there are three groups of ecumaniacs, whom we can code as follows:

NBT—those who will Not Be There

BTB—those who have Been There Before

TFT—those who will be There for the First Time.

Suggestions to the latter two groups should help those in

the first group (which includes most of us) to survive the post-Uppsala, -Nairobi, -Vancouver onslaught.

I. *Ploys for BTB to use on TFT*

a. The informative aside: "On the whole, I'd say (Blake, Potter, or whoever is on deck in 1982/83) is just as able a moderator as 't Hooft was at New Delhi (slight pause, followed by a reminiscent sigh) . . . *or even at Evanston.*"
b. The spurious plea for help: "I can't recall for the moment: On what day did that memorable Hromádka-Dulles debate in '48 at Amsterdam take place?
c. The outright challenge: "Have you ever seen Protopresbyter Borovoi in such good form before?"

II. *All-purpose standard ploy for TFT, to be used in response to any comment by BTB*

"But surely that sort of attitude belongs to the pre-Evanston era of World Council history. I thought they'd buried that once and for all at the 1966 Geneva Conference."

III. *Comments for all delegates to use after their return home, with handy translation guide*

a. "Actually, the little time I spent brushing up on (Swedish, Swahili, British English) paid off handsomely, and I was able to get around (Uppsala, Nairobi, Vancouver) without difficulty."
[TRANSLATION: "All the hotel staff people in (Uppsala, Nairobi, Vancouver) speak the same sort of English I do."]
b. "Philip told me himself, in one of those rare moments when we were able to relax together, that he shared my concern."

71

[TRANSLATION: "I met Dr. Philip Potter, WCC General Secretary, for the first time when I went through the receiving line at the opening reception, and he agreed that it was indeed a hot day even for Kenya."]

c. "The officially adopted statements of the conference are too brief to be lucid."

[TRANSLATION: "The assembly deleted the one paragraph I contributed to our section report."]

d. "The official documents of the conference are far too wordy."

[TRANSLATION: "The assembly voted down my motion to delete all reference to South Africa."]

e. "The (German, French, Indian, Dutch) delegates are remarkably insulated from currents of world opinion."

[TRANSLATION: "One of the (German, French, Indian, Dutch) delegates insisted on speaking (German, French, Tamil, Dutch) in our section instead of English."]

IV. *Ecumenical name-dropping* (including both the quick and the dead)

a. "Paul" (let the context supply either Abrecht, Verghese, St., or Pope, four of the powers behind modern ecumenism.)

b. Instant attention-getter: "I'm the editor-in-chief of *Christianity Today.*"

c. Subtle attention-getter: "Although I was never in the circle of Teilhard's really intimate friends, nevertheless . . ."

d. Sign of being on the in: "Jan Lochman just told me . . ."

V. *Cozying up to the Roman Catholic "observers"*

a. The empathy of shared frustration (during the latter part of the second week): "Discussions like this almost persuade me that an infallible teaching office, functioning *non ex consensu ecclesiae,* is our only hope."

(NOTE: *If spoken in the presence of Protestants as well as Roman Catholics, add the rubric "chuckle" at the end of above quotation.*)

b. Vest-pocket-size translation chart for converting WCC lingo into RC lingo:

Amsterdam, Evanston, New Delhi=
    pre-Vatican II Assemblies
(Swedish, Kenyan, Canadian) police=
    Swiss guard
WCC officials= the Curia
Priesthood of all believers=
    Priesthood of all believers

c. RC allusions the "observers" may appreciate:

Synod of Bishops
Populorum progressio
John Paul II
Barbara Ward (Lady Jackson)
the Dutch Catholics
Philip Scharper
references to the vernacular liturgy

d. Catholic allusions the "observers" may not appreciate:

Vatican I
Apostolicae curae
Unam sanctam
Cardinal Siri
the Dutch Catholics
Cardinal Lefebvre
references to canon law

e. The first two commandments of observer-cultivation:

  (1) Do not try Catholic jokes (e.g., "canon law is the bad side of the good news") until at least the second round in the wee small hours.

  (2) Elbow-bending is better than arm-twisting.[1]

VI. *Points for the all-purpose post- (-Uppsala, -Nairobi, -Vancouver) speech*

  a. Introductory statements. *Instructions:* Choose 1, or 2, or both:

  1. "The most important thing about (Uppsala, Nairobi, Vancouver) was that in an uncertain and chaotic world it took place at all."

  2. "The fact of two weeks of solid human confrontation was more significant than any specific achievement of the assembly."

  NOTE: The beauty of opener 2 is that it permits the speaker to eschew discussion of substantive issues and offer a purely anecdotal account, replete with Ecumenical Name-Dropping (see IV, above).

  b. Description of (Uppsala, Nairobi, Vancouver)'s specific achievements. *Instructions:* Choose 1 or 2, depending upon the audience, but not both, unless it is a very inattentive audience:

  1. For achievements with which the speaker agrees: ". . . represent the distilled wisdom of a quarter of a century of continuous ecumenical reflection . . ."

  2. For achievements with which the speaker disagrees: ". . . the World Council, of course, speaks only *to* the churches and not *for* the churches, and

---

[1] Here is a *really* timeless truth, the quintessence of a lifetime of reflection and action.

its statements have only such authority as its constituent bodies wish to give them . . ."

VII. *Thesis for the inevitable article about (Uppsala, Nairobi, Vancouver) for one's denominational journal.* Instructions: *Choose a or b, but not both*

a. "Some will say that (Uppsala, Nairobi, Vancouver) went too far. I propose to argue, on the contrary, that it did not go nearly far enough."
b. "Some will say that (Uppsala, Nairobi, Vancouver) was too timid. I propose to argue, on the contrary, that it was bold to the point of brashness, venturing into areas where it had no competence to go."

A second set of alternatives. Instructions: *See above.*
a. "The delegates seized on the theme of the assembly with fundamentalistic zeal, proposing wholesale destruction as the only viable basis for a new creation."
b. "Hiding behind their own bourgeois timidity, so typical of the main-line churches they represented, the delegates seemed incapable of taking seriously the radical challenge of the theme of the assembly. As a result, only the old endured."

VIII. *Closing paragraph for speech and/or article*

a. The definitive conclusion: "(Uppsala, Nairobi, Vancouver) is not an end but a beginning."
b. The challenging conclusion: "(Uppsala, Nairobi, Vancouver) marks an important milestone in ecumenical history; it remains for us, in the critical months ahead, to carve a fitting inscription on that milestone." (NOTE: The effect is damp-

ened if the word "tombstone" is inadvertently used.)

MYSTERIOUS PAPAL DOCUMENT DISCOVERED

CURIA CHALLENGES AUTHENTICITY BUT ADRIAN VII BELIEVES IT MAY BE GENUINE

Protestants Pleased

VATICAN CITY, Aug. 15, 1984—A diary that experts claim may have been the heretofore unknown private diary of Pope Paul VI has been found here. The document was discovered as the last of the papal archives were being crated for removal from Vatican City to Geneva, the new location of the office of the Synod of Bishops. Geneva was chosen by Adrian VII, the first married pope.

The new papal Secretary of State, Charles Cardinal Curran, formerly Archbishop of Washington, D.C., stated that Pope Paul may have begun a private diary as long as 25 years ago, having been influenced in his decision to do so by reading an Italian translation of Morris West's *The Shoes of the Fisherman.*

Curia officials, on the other hand, discount the authenticity of the diary, preferring to believe that it was surreptitiously deposited in the Vatican many years ago by West himself. West, currently working on a new novel about the decline of Friday abstinence among the masses, tentatively entitled *No Fish for the Shoe Repair Man,* denied all knowledge of the incident.

Pope Adrian VII, reached in his private quarters on the fourth floor of a slum flat in Rome, where he has been

76

living with his wife and three daughters since his election to the papacy, indicated his belief that the diary might well be genuine. If so, he said, it was certainly in the spirit of a Paul that few outside the Vatican knew well. Pope Adrian was supported in this conjecture by the elderly and conservative Edward Cardinal Schillebeeckx and by the less elderly and less conservative Hans Cardinal Küng, recently appointed head of the Holy Office for the Liquidation of Papal Nuncios. Albert Cardinal Outler, Archbishop of Dallas, Texas, was unavailable for comment.

The diary sheds new light on many aspects of Pope Paul's career. Those who remember the flurry over the Pope's adverse decision on birth control, announced in the summer of 1968, will be interested to discover that Pope Paul not only anticipated the storm of protest that resulted from the now almost forgotten encyclical *Humanae Vitae*, but that he deliberately provoked the violent criticism as an ecumenical gesture to lay to rest Protestant fears about papal power.

Relevant portions of the diary, in an unofficial translation from the Italian, follow, indicating that most of the appraisals made at the time were almost totally unaware of the nuanced subtlety being practiced by the Holy Father in the fateful decree.

"How are We to solve the vexing problem of birth control? We can no longer delay issuing an encyclical in Our name. Such an encyclical will have to fulfill a multitude of functions. It must keep faith with the conservatives for whom a change in teaching would be a cause of scandal. It must allow the progressives to continue their own teaching and practice in this delicate matter, a position now firmly established in the lives of millions of the faithful. It must simultaneously heal the breach between the Holy Catholic Church and those separated from Us in various churches and ecclesial communities, and ensure to heads of state that We have no designs whatever upon their sovereign authority.

"How can these manifold concerns, so dear to the heart of this ancient and venerable See, be encompassed within one document? Clearly, only Our decision to give firm reiteration to the traditional position banning all artificial means of birth control, with no slightest door open for misunderstanding, can satisfy such diverse necessities.

"First, such a statement will instantly satisfy the conservatives, who will find their age-old position vindicated and Our teaching authority saved from the fear of accommodation to worldly considerations.

"Secondly, such an encyclical will be so far removed from the contemporary teaching of great numbers of Our theologians and the de facto practice of Catholic couples that they will find it impossible to obey it; and their public dissent can illustrate that generous latitude of position that must characterize a church truly 'listening to the voice of God in the voice of the times,' which We and the other bishops in solemn assembly at Vatican II so highly lauded.

"Thirdly, because of this benevolent disregard of Our specific recommendations on the part of those within the family of the faithful, the encyclical will assuage once and for all the fears of the 'separated brethren' in diverse churches and ecclesial communities who continue to worry that acceptance of the teaching authority of Our holy office would be binding upon them once they returned to communion with Our ancient and venerable See. Thus Our encyclical will, by deliberate intent, cut the Gordian knot, so-called, that divides the 'separated brethren' from allegiance to Our primal See, since it will be clear that We ask of them no greater acts of obedience to Our teaching than We exact from those presently of Our own household.

"Finally, if in Our encyclical We admonish heads of state to pay no attention to those who wish artificial birth control information or devices to be disseminated amongst their peoples, We will thereby render it impossible for them to accept Our advice without seeming to abdicate the authority of the State and place it once again under the authority of Holy Mother Church, as the bull *Unam Sanctam* by Boniface VIII, of blessed memory, so strenuously avowed. That they will clearly refuse Our suggestion can indicate to all men of goodwill that Our most holy See has no designs whatsoever on regaining the political power and influence it once had."

Late today, Pope Adrian VII appointed a commission of experts to study the document with all of the tools of archaeological research to determine once and for all its authenticity. A report is expected within the decade.

BY PRUDENTIAL HINDSIGHT:

THE DECREE OF THE SACRED CONGREGATION ON THE ORDINATION OF WOMEN

VATICAN CITY (Buenos Aires, Argentina), Jan. 27, 2077— Looked at from the vantage point of a century, the faithful have reason to be grateful for the foresight and wisdom that guided the Sacred Congregation for the Doctrine of the Faith in January 1977 to deny ordination of women to the priesthood. What has been impressive in the interval has been the resolute willingness of the church to follow to the end the logic that inspired the original document, once its lapidary consequences began to unfold.

It will be remembered that it was only a few years after the promulgation of the document in question that the church was called upon to elect a new pope. Reflecting upon the truth enshrined in the document of the Sacred Congregation that "Jesus Christ did not call any *woman* to become part of the Twelve" (italics added), it occurred to one of the members of the College of Cardinals, meeting in Rome in 1978, that a further step in the ever-unfolding amplitude of divine truth could be deduced by the substitution of only one word, viz., "Jesus Christ did not call any Italian to become part of the Twelve" (Italians deleted).

This eminently reasonable deduction persuaded a majority of the college that the time was ripe to look beyond the Apennines for a new Vicar of Christ. In a move held by some to be "a break with tradition," and by others to be "a restoration of the purity of the early church," in 1978 the first non-Italian pope in over 400 years was elected. Once such a precedent was set, the next conclave had little difficulty in substituting the word "European" for the word "Italian," so that in 1984 the cardinals chose Augustine I, a black African who, with good reason, took the name of an earlier father of the church sharing with him the same skin color and geographical point of origin.[1]

It was a scant twenty years later, in 2004, that the next pope promulgated an initially controversial decree changing the style of vestments for priests officiating at Mass. Citing the Sacred Congregation's statement (a) that there must be a "natural resemblance" between the one who celebrates and the maleness of Christ, and noting (b) that the one who celebrates must be clearly and easily discernible as a man (since "[if] such [were not the] case it would be difficult to see in the minister the image of Christ. For Christ Himself was and remains a man"), His Holiness decreed (c) that all lace, skirts, and similar finery should be abolished, and (d) that priests should henceforth wear trousers so that their masculinity would never be in doubt. (The fact that in the year 2004 trousers were still held to be distinctively masculine attire indicates that the "signs of the times" were not being discerned with full sensitivity by the Vatican.)

Much more far-reaching was a papal decision issued on Jan. 6, 2044, on the fortieth anniversary of the vestment decree, and therefore called *Quadragesimo Anno II.* This statement, taking encyclical form (and therefore becoming much more difficult to undo) argued that since Christ was a man and all priests should be men, a logical extension of the argument necessarily implied that since Christ was a Jew, all priests should be Jews.

The far-reaching consequences of this encyclical can be

---

[1] It is clear that this account and the previous one cannot be reconciled by any of the existing tools of historical scholarship. There was a similar *contretemps* at the time of the Babylonian Captivity. All we can do is wait until 1984 and see if the pope is named Adrian or Augustine. [Ed.]

imagined, for despite the most assiduous blandishments offered by Vatican Radio Free World combined with the advertising skills of the Paulist Fathers, priestly vocations immediately dropped to zero and stayed at that point with rigid consistency. No success whatever was achieved in trying to persuade young Jewish males to enter diocesan seminaries. Only the most nuanced arguments by a generation of canon lawyers, constructing an argument on the statement of Pius XI, of blessed memory —i.e., "Spiritually we are all Semites"—furnished a theologically satisfactory justification for readmitting to the spiritually oriented priesthood those of the Gentile persuasion.

The truly critical point, however, as all remember well, occurred when the next pontiff, a native of Latin America (who had spent most of his active priesthood as a political prisoner), invoked the notorious *Limitación de tres años* (which, in rough translation, we might render as "the three-year limitation"). As with all the previous documents, the line of reasoning was impeccable, devastating as were the results of the argument to the apostolic priesthood.

Reminding the faithful that in terms of the original 1977 document, admission to the priesthood involved an identification with Christ beyond the possibility of confusion, His Holiness O'Higgins I decreed that there would be a "limitation of three years" on a priest's time of public ministry, this being the maximum time that Christ could have spent in a similar calling. The new Pope broadly hinted, though he did not explicitly decree (the time not yet being ripe), that death at the hands of the state would be the most appropriate way to terminate such a public ministry, thus bearing witness in unmistakable fashion to the "natural resemblance" between Christ and his followers.

The *Limitación de tres años* (the "three-year limitation") was, of course, the direct cause of the Crisis of 2076, from which we are just emerging, since all of the priests who had served over three years or who were over the age of 33 (whichever came first) felt obliged to hand in their resignations, which were received and accepted in the nick of time by the Pope, who was himself forced to abdicate by the logic of his own decree—small wonder, since he was 83 at the time.

This "housecleaning" (as the Protestant press rather unkindly described it) means that there is now no College of Cardinals, no Curia (an institution that had survived even the earlier translation of the Vatican from Rome to Buenos Aires), no bishops, and only a handful of priests, many of whom, due to the length of seminary training, were already approaching the new retirement age.

Sensing the need for some sort of governing body, the remaining priests established a small body which they called an "apostolic college," and decided that they would share the rule among themselves. Sensing that their rate of rotation into retirement would soon exceed their ability to secure replacements by ordinary measures, they decided that the whole question of who should belong to the "college"—or (to put it another way) who should be ordained, for how long, and to what end—was worthy of reexamination. The decision was easily reached, once it was pointed out that the Congregation's decree of 1977 was not infallible and thus was, by definition, "fallible," and could consequently be reexamined. The action effectively nullified, or at least reduced to the state of a pious opinion, the decree of 1977, so that the whole matter could receive fresh discussion.

We can see, therefore, how rash was the opinion of those a mere century ago (a fleeting instant, as Mother Church [sic] measures time) who felt that the church was saying "no" to women's ordination. The very decree that seemed to shut the door can now be seen, by prudential hindsight, to have been the key that opened it. We can look back on it with gratitude, pondering the mysterious workings of the Spirit, as we prepare our hearts and minds for the solemn coronation next Tuesday of Pope Joan I, née Kathleen O'Houlihan of the Bronx, New York 10458.

ECUMENICAL SENSITIVITY PERCEPTION
(E.S.P.)

WHAT the ecumenical movement needs is more E.S.P., or Ecumenical Sensitivity Perception. Problem: How can we indicate to one another who we really are, without lowering ourselves to the crassness of using words? The Roman Catholics have an answer other Christian bodies might well adopt. They place clarifying initials after the names of their key theologians, thus giving others a hint of what to expect. If one encounters a theologian with an O.P. after his name, for example, the chances are pretty good that he is a Thomist unless he comes from Holland, in which case the chances are pretty good that he is in trouble. If he sports an S.J., we treat him differently from an O.S.B. (We don't ask O.S.B.'s about "black popes"; nor do we complain to them that "The new liturgy has lost its medieval grandeur.") We know that if the theologian has an S.S. he will probably be training Catholic seminarians, while if he has an O. Carm. he will probably be training Protestant seminarians and be named Roland Murphy.

Protestants might emulate this custom as an ecumenical gesture to others. What does a Protestant D.D. indicate to a Catholic, except that the degree is unearned? What help is a tag like B.D. or S.T.M., when such degrees can mean all things to all men—a fine tactic when one is in Rome, save that one usually isn't. What we need, if ecumenical sensitivity perception is to become a two-way street, is a series of initials available to Protestants that will telegraph their viewpoint quickly to Catholics. The following represents only the bare bones of such a proposal:

O.S.L.—the Order of St. Longinus. Since all Protestant observers at Vatican II sat in the tribune of St. Longinus, the initials O.S.L. can be a shorthand way of stating, "I was at the Vatican Council and I'm Very Open." Subtle gradations within the order can include O.S.L.f.m. (one of the friars minor, i.e., one who was present for less than the aggregate of one full session), and O.S.L.F.M. (Friar Major, or one who was present at every minute of all four sessions, a designation legitimately placed only after the name of Douglas Horton.)

F.O.F.P.—a way of indicating the ultimate in ecumenical and economic cooperation, a "Fish on Friday Protestant," i.e., one who is going to keep the fishing industry afloat during the transition period when Catholics are not yet psychologically able to eat fish on Friday voluntarily. The opposite of F.O.F.P. would be an F.O.F.C., or "Fish on Friday Catholic," i.e., a traditionalist who refuses to come to terms with the realities of the modern world.

D.O.G. Theol.—an honorary degree, granted by Emory University, indicating that one is a Death of God Theologian.

Tüb. Theol.—a self-awarded degree communicating the information, "I did some graduate work in theology at Tübingen. . . . Well, at least I visited there one Wednesday evening and heard Hans Küng give a lecture." The overtones of "Tüb" may also suggest (a) something about cleaning up the mess in Rome, Geneva, Canterbury, or (for the politically conscious) Washington; or (b) that one is named Tom Driver.

P.F.—shorthand for "Peanuts Forever!" communicating the following: "My children's sermons start Where People Are."

Q.T.L. or Q.F.L.—indications of one's academic achievements, standing respectively for "Qualified in two (or three) languages," and "Qualified in four (or five) languages." When spoken, they must be inflected with enough assurance to indicate that the option contained within the parentheses is the correct one.

S.A.—omnibus initials available for a series of interchangeable referents, each of which means the same thing, viz., Selma, Ala. (or, I Was There, Why Weren't You?), Saul Alinsky (or, I Believe Conflict Can Be Creative; If You Don't, Let's Have A Confrontation), or simply, for the chaste, and old-fashioned, Social Action. Those who infer that such varieties of S.A. mean Secular Agnostic are merely letting their biases show. Those who infer that Sex Appeal is meant may be right.

Note to seminarians: special identification will be needed, such as G.U.T.S. (graduate, Union Theological Seminary) and G.O.D. (graduate of Drew), but such honors must be worn lightly enough to avoid the charge of hubris that those not eligible for such identifying tags may visit upon those who are.

Most seminarians, however, will simply want to indicate their own theological identification, and a new degree is suggested to attain this end: B.D., e.g., (depending upon one's taste) Barth devotee, Bultmann devotee, Brunner devotee, Berdyaev devotee, Baillie (John) devotee, Baillie (Donald) devotee, Bennett devotee, Bonhoeffer devotee, Buri devotee, Balthasar devotee, Buber devotee, Bulgakov devotee, Brightman devotee. Such designation will immediately enable the unwary Catholic to spot the theological predilections of those with whom he is dealing.

S.N.C.C.—this is not a statement of achievement, but a slogan for the future. It reads "Slander No Contemporary Christian" and is a theological equivalent of the eleventh commandment of the G.O.P. (God's Own People), "Thou shalt not speak ill of a fellow Republican."

St. Hereticus, S.J.[1]

ECCLESIASTICISM
"THE EASY, FUN WAY"

THE Catholics have come up with a game called *Merit*. Modeled on *Monopoly*, it "teaches children and adults Catholicism the easy, fun way." The manufacturers promise, "Everyone will *beg* to play the only *game* ever to receive ecclesiastical approbation."

You get 700 merits to start with, a card indicating that you have been baptized, and a plastic statuette—for example, Mary, Joseph, an angel, or Jesus. The purpose of the game (and the purpose, obviously, of Catholicism) is to acquire property, build churches, and get Home with six of the seven sacraments. In building structures, as *The National Catholic Reporter* comments, "Foreign Missions can't be built till the convent and seminary are built, just as St. Paul taught."

The questions give you a chance to learn what makes A Good Catholic. If you draw a card that asks, "Is there more than one true church?" you must answer, "No, there is only one true church, and that is the Catholic Church."

All this for only $12.50. ("Get ready for peak Easter, First Communion, and Confirmation Sales!" exhorts an ad in the *Specialty Salesman*.)

---

[1] Separated Journalist.

Since such a gesture has come from the Catholic side, ecumenical courtesy suggests that a corresponding gesture come from Protestants. Could there not be a Protestant game that is just as typical of Protestantism as *Merit* is of Catholicism?

There not only could be, there is. I have just invented it. The Protestant counterpart of *Merit* is called *I Protest*. It is a bit more complicated since it must be manufactured in many editions, each of which contains different answers to the same questions. Before the game begins, each player has to make a number of preliminary decisions. If he is an Episcopalian, he has to decide whether to be High, Low, Broad, or UAC (ultra Anglo-Catholic). If Presbyterian, will he be Northern, Southern, Conservative, Bible, or Cumberland? A Baptist must choose between Southern, American, Free Will, or Two-Seed-in-the-Spirit, and having made that decision, must further determine whether to be Militantly Anti-Ecumenical (the easiest choice) or Just The Least Bit Ecumenically Inclined (entailing an automatic loss of two turns before he can get into the game).

Denominational affiliation determined, the player must then select a theological stance. Since there is absolutely no correlation between a denominational affiliation and a theological stance, a new set of choices is required. On standard models of *I Protest*, the following options are possible: liberal, conservative, ultraconservative, fundamentalist, sectarian, neo-orthodox, Bultmannian, or "God is dead." Thus one could be a liberal Presbyterian, a "God is dead" Episcopalian (a popular option these days), or a Bultmannian Congregationalist.

The statuettes are then chosen, depending on the ETQ (Ecclesiastical-Theological Quotient) the players have determined for themselves. All Episcopalians have bishops (borrowed from any nearby chess set, or available at no extra cost in deluxe models); and depending on the highness or lowness of their ETQ, they will affix either plastic clerical collars or neckties to their figurines. Baptists are given miniature bathtubs, symbolizing total immersion, while Congregationalists receive watering cans to proclaim that sprinkling is enough. Presbyterians choose, according to their ETQ, a statue of Eugene Carson Blake, Donald Shriver, or John Fry. Methodists receive shattered wine glasses, indicating that drinking is o-u-t for Christians, while Lutherans get overflowing beer mugs, symbolizing *Gemütlichkeit*, the Munich Oktoberfest, and all that sort of thing.

The game begins as each player draws a card and answers the question on it. Here is where things begin to get difficult. For the right answer in *I Protest* cannot be found by consulting some counterpart of the Baltimore Catechism. It must be determined by correlating the various factors entering into the player's ETQ. (In order to speed things up, a small computer is included with the deluxe models, or is available for rent at $179.50 per evening.)

A simple question such as "Is there anything wrong in having a cocktail before dinner?" gets a straightforward answer from a straightforward Episcopalian ("No"), or a straightforward Methodist ("Yes"); but when other factors are programmed into the answer, decisions become more complex. What, for example, is the answer to the question, "Is C.O.C.U. a good idea?" when the player is a liberal Southern Presbyterian who attended a conservative Southern Baptist Bible Belt college but married a low-church Episcopalian from Virginia who believes that bishops are only of the *bene esse* of the church? Only the computer knows.

Suppose, however, as frequently happens, that the computer's answer is unacceptable. In this case, the player draws from a second pile of cards labeled "Sola Scriptura," on which he or she will find a Bible text clarifying what his or her position as a Protestant (relying on the authority of Scripture) should be. Should the verse prove ambiguous ("Whither thou goest, I will go," for example, could mean all sorts of things vis-à-vis C.O.C.U.), the player has a number of further options:

a. If he[1] has declared himself a fundamentalist, he simply shouts the verse loudly over and over again until the other players resignedly let him move his counter.

b. If he is a liberal, he turns the question over to The Exegetes (a group of any three players who retire to ponder the matter indefinitely).

c. If he is an ecumaniac (defined as "a Christian who loves all branches of Christendom better than his own"), he will draw from a third pile of cards for further enlightenment. This pile is labeled "Tradition" and consists of quotations from St. Augustine, St. Anselm, St. John (Calvin), Pascal, Kierkegaard, Teresa of Avila, and H. Jackson Forstman. By collating the inspired Biblical text and the rich resources of Tradition, the player can usually arrive at a satisfactory answer.

Should the latter *still* not be possible, the game goes into a new phase in which all the players discuss the matter in rigid parliamentary fashion. In the Presbyterian version of *I Protest*, this phase is called General Assembly; in the Episcopalian, it is General Convention. Only antiecumaniacs will insist on calling it Vatican Council.

Resources are not yet exhausted should a stalemate once again ensue, for if this happens, a further procedure

---

[1]This time the sexist language is that of Hereticus himself, a regrettable lapse, but a lapse nonetheless. As a monument to the times in which the original essay was written (1966), I have let it stand. [Ed.]

can be employed, the only procedure common to all versions of *I Protest*. This procedure is entitled Appointing a Committee to Consider the Matter and Report at the Next Annual Meeting.

It is now the second player's move.

But this description has not yet gotten to the real heart of *I Protest,* the move (always available to every player) that most truly depicts the genius of Protestantism. Anytime a player becomes dissatisfied with the course of the game or even with the rules, he or she can draw from the largest pile of cards on the whole board, labeled "The Right of Private Judgment." The disgruntled player simply says, "I appeal to The Right of Private Judgment," draws a card, reads from it whatever move he or she wishes, makes it, and motions to the next player to take his or her turn. (Each card is blank, but nobody else knows this ahead of time.)

Since there is no court of appeal higher than The Right of Private Judgment, the other players must either accept the player's decision or vote to Withdraw Recognition. Should they do this, the player thus discriminated against says loudly and prophetically, "I Protest," withdraws his or her counter from the board, and Starts Another Denomination. This is done by merely spinning the counter until he gets a 2 and a 3 in succession, knowing that where two or three are gathered together, it is legitimate to have an Organizational Meeting.

The player who starts the Most New Denominations in the course of an evening is The Winner.

Recipe: Take One Portion of Religion and One of Politics; Mix Well

BOYLE'S LAW REVISED

BOYLE'S LAW:

At any given temperature the volume of a given mass of gas varies inversely as the pressure to which it is subjected.

—Named for Robert Boyle, 1627–1691, who formulated it.

REV. EUGENE BOYLE, a Roman Catholic priest in California, is running for the state assembly. Not a very new thing in the world of the Fr. Drinans, the Andrew Youngs, and such. But in this case, there has been an interesting twist, and occasion has been provided for the restatement of a venerable doctrine. The Archbishop of San Francisco has removed Fr. Boyle's faculties to preach, as long as he is a candidate. Fr. Boyle can still say Mass, hear confession, and do all the other things priests do when they are not running for public office and have all their faculties intact.

But preach? Never. Never on Sunday. The archdiocesan newspaper tells why:

> The rationale behind this, according to the Archdiocesan Information Office, is that preaching aims to unite the People of God, whereas politics in the pulpit is divisive. For the sake of the people, the faculties to preach have been withdrawn in this case. Were this candidate to expand his preaching faculties in the pulpit to politics, then logic would suggest other candidates for the office he seeks should have the same privilege. (*The Monitor*, Feb. 14, 1974, p. 9)

At last! In all the difficult years of public dispute about "religion and politics," we have been waiting for a clear and definite "rationale" (as *The Monitor* describes it) as to why politics should be kept out of the pulpit. The rationale has now been given, and it is simple and unblushingly straightforward: "Preaching aims to unite the People of God, whereas politics in the pulpit is divisive."

This, naturally, is no more than a reiteration of what the church has always taught, but it has significant contemporary implications:

1. Imagine the consequences if politics *were* allowed in the pulpit. It might then happen that at some future time (which may God forbid) a priest would get up in the pulpit and call attention to upcoming abortion legislation, urging his people to take a particular stand on it as a result of their Christian consciences. That would be politics-in-the-pulpit with a vengeance. But we may rest assured that such unwarranted political intrusion will not occur, thanks to the all-embracing instructions of the chancery office. Again: Imagine the scandal to the faithful that would have ensued if at any time in the past priests had preached about birth control or movie censorship. Yet again: Imagine the scandal to the faithful that would have ensued if a cardinal (whether in New

York or elsewhere) had mentioned the war in Vietnam or had used his pulpit to urge support for federal aid to parochial school education. Such political intrusions would have been divisive indeed, and totally out of keeping with the instructions issued to Fr. Boyle.

2. The proscription against politics in the pulpit is given, we quote, "for the sake of the people." How wise, in this era of mass propaganda, to avoid propaganda at Mass! Since Americans are really children (as The Leader in Washington has said so well), they need protection from rude ideas. They need to be assured that the cares of the outside world will not follow them into church. Nonpolitical preaching can comfort the afflicted, but political preaching might afflict the comfortable, which would defeat the purposes of churchgoing.

3. We see abundant evidence that, as the rationale states, nonpolitical preaching aims "to unite the People of God." Examples abound. No priest would ever urge attendance at Thursday night Bingo in ways that might divide his congregation. No pastor would ever refer to the parable of the sheep and the goats in such a way that his flock [sic] could doubt for a moment on which side of the divide they all belonged. No pulpiteer would ever suggest that the People of God might be divided if some of them attended certain cinematic diversions for reasons of prurient interest.

So the principle that politics does not belong in the pulpit, as the church has always taught and practiced, is once again affirmed. And Fr. Boyle, dutiful son of the church that he is, has agreed not to preach in church while he is a candidate. As he put it, in what might be called an example of candor, the ban "will limit me very little. . . . Most of my preaching has been done in the streets and marketplaces, which is where Christianity began anyhow."

This riposte suggests a limitation to the Archbishop's victory. For preaching "in the streets and marketplaces" does sound a little dangerous. This is the sort of thing St. Paul used to do, the final result of which was to undermine the Roman Way of Life. Indeed, the crowds that used to listen to his sermons became known as "the upsetters of the world" (Acts 17:6). Fr. Boyle, in other words, is actually better off than he was before. The only really effective way the Archbishop could have muzzled him would have been to *forbid him to preach anywhere except in the pulpit.* This would have kept him out of controversial "streets and marketplaces" and deprived him of his most sympathetic hearers. For with the way church attendance is going these days, the least likely time and place for a controversial idea to catch fire politically is at Mass on Sunday morning.

BOYLE'S LAW REVISED:

In any given controversy, the effectiveness of the one muzzled is increased proportionately in relation to the pressure from higher up to which he is subjected.
—*Named for Eugene Boyle,* fl. *1974, who exemplified it.*

JOHN MITCHELL, THEOLOGIAN; OR,
 ON GETTING ONE THING
 PERFECTLY CLEAR
 ABOUT THE DEVIL

LET it never be said that I was the one who first introduced religion into politics. I am, of course, part of a long theological tradition that says that religion and politics do not mix. Consequently, if I do not introduce politics into religion, no more should politicians introduce religion into politics. But when they do, as John Mitchell, once Attorney General of the United States, used to do, it becomes necessary to comment.

Actually John was beaten to the draw by his wife, who several years earlier had urged that Senator Fulbright be "crucified," a favorite theological method for getting rid of one's opponents. Her husband emerged as a lay theologian, in the course of a speech to the Women's National Republican Club. Trying to stifle rumors that the Justice Department had dismissed an antitrust suit against the International Telephone and Telegraph Corporation in return for ITT help in underwriting San Diego as the site of the Republican convention, theologian Mitchell said: "There is about as much connection with the ITT antitrust suit and the Republican convention going to San Diego as there is between the Lord and the devil."

Mr. Mitchell, the *politician*, was suggesting that there was no connection between a favorable settlement by the Justice Department vis-à-vis ITT and a lot of money pouring into Republican coffers from ITT. But Mr. Mitchell, the *theologian*, did not quite bring it off. For the Lord and the devil, in traditional theology, have actually been much closer than he seems to understand.

As Martin Luther, a theologian who occasionally dabbled in politics, liked to say: "The devil is God's devil." The devil, Luther insisted, is free to roam only to the degree that God lets him,[1] and God keeps him on a leash so that he can't get too far afield and muck things up too badly. Another tradition, much earlier than Luther, tells us that the devil is really a fallen angel and that he was thus once privy to all that went on in the heavenly councils.

---

[1] Here is one place where sexist language seems appropriate. [Ed.]

95

In the book of Job we even read about God and the devil working out what (in the Washington parlance Mr. Mitchell loves) could be called a "deal." God is very pleased with his servant Job. But Satan, who is present at one of the meetings of the "sons of God" [*sic*], challenges the degree of Job's commitment, with the result that God tells Satan he can do anything he wants to Job except take his life. "All that he has is in your power" is God's way of delegating authority to Satan. Pretty close connection.

Then, of course, we have those crucial conversations between Jesus and the devil in which it is revealed that they are on intimate terms, each knowing the other's strengths and weaknesses. They swap Scripture verses and engage in three significant theological discussions. The devil knows a lot about such themes as "messiahship," and Jesus knows a lot about the tricks the devil has up his sleeve. Jesus wins each encounter, and so the devil leaves him—but only "until an opportune time," according to Luke.

Thus it is clear, even from as cursory a treatment as the above, that "the Lord and the devil" are on pretty close terms with each other. If the connection between an ITT antitrust suit and the Republican convention going to San Diego is only as close as the connection "between the Lord and the devil," we can assume that the connection is very close indeed.

That disposes of one problem. Mr. Mitchell, the *theologian*, is telling us that one could hardly conceive of the Republican convention in San Diego and the settling of the ITT antitrust suit being any closer than they actually are. His imagery of God and the devil is redolent of conversations, long relationships, and "deals." So far so clear.

But there is one matter Mr. Mitchell has not yet

cleared up for us, and we must eagerly await his next theological pronouncement. In the Biblical accounts it is clear that God has control over the devil rather than the devil having control over God. It is not yet clear in Mr. Mitchell's script who plays which part. Does the Justice Department finally crack the whip over ITT, or does ITT finally call the shots against the Justice Department? Which one is in charge—government or big business? Who controls whom? It will be fascinating to know how our new theologian answers that one.

Then, of course, we can get down to the really interesting theological question: How can we dethrone not only devils but also false gods? I'm eager to bow the knee neither to the Justice Department nor to ITT, particularly when they are reported to be no closer to one another than "the Lord and the devil." That's much too close for comfort.

A NEW APPROACH TO AMNESTY;
OR, HELP FROM AN UNEXPECTED SOURCE

ONCE upon a time, back in the days when the country had a duly elected Vice President, that Vice President (whose name was once a household word but now escapes me)[1] used to speak very firmly about law and order and the need for people to pay publicly for their misdeeds. He was particularly hard on young men who felt that it was wrong to kill Southeast Asians and who went either to jail or to Canada to avoid having to do so. The

---

[1] Diligent research has uncovered that Hereticus' consistent memory lapse throughout the essay is a reference to Spiro T. Who. [Ed.]

Vice President, whose name escapes me, thought such people should be severely punished; indeed, he felt that a dozen fine young Americans going off to kill Southeast Asians were worth more than all the thousands of effete Americans who refused to do so.

But one day it turned out that the Vice President whose name escapes me hadn't been particularly careful about obeying the law himself. Not only had he been receiving illegal payoffs and feathering his own nest during the time those fine young Americans were killing Southeast Asians, but he was charged with about forty other crimes as well, crimes that ordinarily would have sent him to jail for many years—for many *more* years, in fact, than young men accused of not killing Southeast Asians could be sent to jail.

Problem: What should be done to a Vice President who says that *other* people who break the law should pay to the hilt, when it turns out that he *himself* has broken many more laws than they are accused of breaking?

In balmier times, one of the Vice President's closest friends, an Attorney General who himself later came under indictment for breaking other laws and whose name also escapes me,[2] said about Government officials, "Watch not what we say but what we do." This is the best possible advice for understanding the Vice President whose name escapes me. For what he *did* when he was accused of breaking very clear laws was rather different from what he *said* should be done to other people who were accused of breaking very questionable laws: He worked out a "deal" with some people in the Government who were not yet under indictment.

1. He agreed to resign from his job.

[2]Intensive research has uncovered that this is the subject of the previous essay. [Ed.]

2. He agreed to plead guilty to a "lesser charge" in exchange for not being prosecuted on forty more serious charges.

3. He agreed to pay a token fine and accept symbolic probation.

In return for this, those people in the Government who were not yet under indictment did the following:

1. They agreed to let him send mail free for a month and have a uniformed chauffeur and limousine at his disposal.

2. They agreed to give him fifteen minutes of free TV time to tell everybody that he was really innocent.

3. They agreed to forget about all the other charges and never, never bring them up in federal court.

Here is an admirable solution to the vexing amnesty question of what to do with the "draft dodgers." We simply transfer the procedures used against major criminals like the Vice President whose name escapes me to draft dodgers who, it will probably turn out, aren't even minor criminals.

Thus: Amnesty case #69427F.   Walsh, Frederick, age 23, living in Canada. "Crime": refusing four years ago for reasons of conscience to kill Southeast Asians. Walsh, loyally following the example of the former Vice President whose name escapes me, does the following:

1. He agrees to resign from his present job (short-order cook at an all-night diner in central Manitoba).

2. He agrees to plead guilty to a "lesser charge" (a traffic violation for illegal parking in a Toledo school playground back in 1967).

3. He agrees to pay a token fine (14¢) and accept symbolic probation (telling the junior high school principal once a year for three years that he won't do it again).

In return, those members of the Government not yet

under indictment do the following:

1. They agree to let him send free mail to all his friends in Canada for a month and offer him a uniformed chauffeur (an offer, Walsh says, "I could refuse").

2. They agree to give him fifteen minutes of free TV time to explain to the nation why he is innocent of any crime, since the "law" ordering him to go to Vietnam was illegal.

3. They agree to forget all about the other charges and never, never bring them up in federal court.

Here is where the analogy begins to limp. The ideal script would call for putting the *Government* on probation, directing all its officials not yet under indictment to check in daily with the young men of conscience whose "crime" was to have been right about the war's wrongness before anybody else. If the Government officials who are not yet under indictment listened to people like that, trust might one day be restored. Even in Washington.

Insights from the Military Way of Life

A NEW STRATEGY
FOR PACIFISTS

> WASHINGTON, D.C.—The Navy is proposing to spend more than $700 million producing a new eight-inch gun that the General Accounting Office contends is so inaccurate at longer ranges that it would use up all its ammunition before hitting a target.
> —*The New York Times*

PACIFISTS have had an understandable reluctance to support military appropriations bills. They have sensed, probably rightly, a possible discrepancy between their own aims and those of the Pentagon.

The above information, however, suggests the need for a change in tactics. Rather than *opposing* military spending, it may now become the duty of every pacifist to *support* expenditures for precisely the kind of weapons described above. If our nation's military experts are committed to designing weapons incapable of hitting their targets, we may well be on the way to a warless world.

Cost is no problem. Seven hundred million dollars is a small price to pay for having battleships with guns that will be unable to hit their targets. The axiom is unassailable: targets that cannot be hit are targets that will survive, a goal dear to the heart of every pacifist.

To enlist the support of the military to ensure the

success of the pacifist enterprise is not too high a compromise for even the most single-minded antimilitarist. "Make friends for yourselves," the greatest peacemaker of all told his followers, "by the mammon of unrighteousness." What mammon is more unrighteous than the billions in the Pentagon budget?

Indeed, one need not even be deceitful (the "wise as serpents" routine) in the cause of a higher righteousness; one can simply let the script play itself out. In the story cited above, for example, the General Accounting Office stated that "one eight-inch gun will expend all of its ammunition" trying to hit targets at a distance of more than 10 miles, though the gun is designed for a range of 20 miles. Yet when faced with these dismal statistics, Vice Admiral James H. Doyle, Jr., Vice Chief of Naval Operations for Surface Warfare, stoutly maintained that the new weapon was proving to be, as he put it, "a fine gun." This type of appraisal should bring joy to the heart of every card-carrying member of the Fellowship of Reconciliation and the Catholic Peace Fellowship. Indeed, Vice Admiral Doyle should be given an honorary membership in both organizations, since he has enunciated an axiom common to both groups: a fine gun is a gun that will not work.

The principle the U.S. Navy is exemplifying in this episode—that money should be spent on weapons that will not hit their targets—could be expanded to other areas of the military as well. Two examples suggest themselves:

1. A bomber could be designed that would be a model of perfection in its radar-scanning equipment, its retractable landing gear, and its radio-interception sensibility, but would have an engine that was incapable of lifting the plane off the ground whenever it was loaded with bombs. Once such planes were built with military funds,

they could be taken over by the taxpayers, and used for civilian purposes such as flying serum to plague-infested areas or transporting groups of school children to other parts of the world for three-week friendship exchanges.

2. It would also be worthwhile investing in rifles that could ingest bullets but not disgorge them. An intricate loading mechanism could be contracted for over a five-year period with a cost escalation limited to, say, $7 billion, after which, but only after which, it could be noted that bullets so loaded could not be fired without destroying (a) the mechanism, (b) the rifle, and (c) the operator of the rifle, in that order. While the Army, in the interests of national defense, might consider all three items expendable, in that order, the number of young men signing up for a volunteer army using such weapons could be expected to phase out to absolute zero, once the word began to get around.

We have always been told that the best way to ensure peace is to increase the military budget. Thanks to the Navy's engineers, it looks at long last as though the argument is unassailable.

TURNING THE (TIDE) TABLES

American military personnel have trained dolphins, who will not willingly kill members of their species, to swim into the hulls of enemy ships with explosives strapped to their snouts, and to nuzzle enemy divers with hypodermic syringes filled with pressurized carbon dioxide, causing the divers to explode.

—*News item*

Fragment Discovered Long After the Great Flood of 1994,
Waterlogged, but Still Decipherable

THE BOOK OF HEXODUS

CHAPTER 9

1 And it came to pass in those days that the Lord God, looking at her creation and the way her human creatures had missed the point, 2 caused a tidal wave to sweep across the face of the earth, thus putting creation back to the second day. 3 And on this occasion raised she up no Noah to build him an ark. But so great was her compassion for her children that she caused a deep sleep to come upon them, 4 and while they slumbered, behold, she gave them gills instead of lungs, so that they could survive in the new environment which the Lord their God had planned for them.

5 And behold, all the human beings found themselves presented for judgment before the throne of the Great Dolphin of the Deep, who spoke to them on this wise: 6 Verily, I say unto thee that in thy world thou tookest the dolphins, dwellers in the sea, 7 and attempted to impose on them the ways of dwellers on the land. 8 But now the tide tables are turned, and thou, who attempted to form us in thine image of destructiveness, art required to be re-formed in our image of gentleness, since we now have the upper fin.

9 Therefore hearken unto the commandments before which thou shalt be held accountable in the deep and the shallow places of the sea that are now thy dwelling.

10 A new commandment give I unto thee, not as the world giveth, a commandment thou hast not heard before, which goeth on this wise: 11 Thou shalt not kill. 12 Yet another commandment give I unto thee (having

observed thine attempts to train our dolphinfolk to kill, nuzzling underwater divers with syringes filled with carbon dioxide): [13] Thou shalt not bear false witness. Thou shalt not lie, either by word or deed; thy yea shall be yea and thy nay nay, or [14] it shall not go well with thee in the Great Deep. [15] Be it known that I say unto thee even this as well: Thou shalt not teach others to kill. For as we dolphins do not kill one another, [16] neither do we kill humankind. Therefore (in an exquisite reversal of justice) we decree that thou shalt not only not kill dolphins, but [17] Thou shalt not kill thine own kind, either.

[18] In thy former life above the water, thou seemedst never content with what thou hadst, even though there was enough for all. [19] So I charge thee in this new life: [20] Thou shalt not covet thy neighbors' sandbars, nor their estuaries, nor their freshwater tributaries, nor their coral reefs, nor any things that are thy neighbors'. [21] The sea is vast, there is enough and to spare for all, so rest content. [22] For if not, it shall not go well with thee in the Great Deep.

CHAPTER 10

[1] All this I sum up for thee in our great commandment (obviously unknown to thee); [2] Thou shalt love thy neighbor as thyself. [3] And if anyone, seeking to justify himself or herself, should ask, And who is my neighbor? mark well the answer: [4] Whosoever swimmeth by. [5] And if, perchance, that meaning should escape thee, hearken well to the story told in an old sea-chantey:

[6] A certain fish was going from the Bahama Banks to the Grand Banks, [7] and as he was traversing the Bermuda Triangle, behold, a band of sharks waylaid him, bit him in divers places, partially de-scaled him, and departed, leaving him half dead. [8] Whole schools of tuna

and whitefish went by ignoring him, muttering, Luck of the draw! Law of the sea! ⁹ Then an eel chanced by, stopped, gave the fish a slight shock to revivify him, and coiling herself about him, drew him inch by inch to a small cove where, safe from further bands of marauding sharks, he could recover. ¹⁰ And offering a small gratuity to the octopus guarding the cove, she said, ¹¹ Look after him well, and, if perchance this sum is not sufficient, I, when I return, will further recompense thee with a choice morsel garnered from the harbor floor.

12 Who, then, was neighbor to him who fell among sharks? ¹³ To which the humans, standing as they were before the bar of judgment, and realizing that they were on the spot, could only reply, ¹⁴ She who looked after him. ¹⁵ To which the Great Dolphin of the Deep replied, Now thou knowest how to comport thyself in this new realm. ¹⁶ Attend, therefore, unto the doing of it.

Foibles of Our Time

(With apologies to James Thurber,
Fables for Our Time)

SITUATION ETHICS

FRITZ and Heinrich were creeping up stealthily on the enemy field headquarters under cover of a cloudy, moonless night. As they inched along the ground they suddenly encountered an unexpected obstacle for which their previous reconnaissance briefings had not prepared them. Fritz cursed softly to himself, muttering that it was too dark to see whether or not the obstacle was a land mine. He continued to inch ahead, however, and was soon beyond it. Heinrich felt it important to investigate the matter carefully and lit a small candle from his emergency kit, in order to make sure that he was not about to activate an explosive device left there by the enemy.

The sudden illumination attracted the attention of an alert sentry stationed in front of the enemy field headquarters, who immediately drew a bead on the light and dispatched nine bullets in the space of five eighths of a second.

MORAL: *Sometimes it is better to curse the darkness than to light a candle.*

THE CHILD WHO HAD TO HAVE THINGS

There once was a family that seemed to be pretty well fixed. Each member had sufficient food, clothing, education, and leisure time. Even their radio was, for that era, a marvel of efficiency. But one day the son came home from grade school saying, "Somebody has invented a radio that shows pictures. We simply *must* have one." And lo, in the light of such heartfelt necessity, a television set was purchased.

A few years later the same son came home from high school saying, "Somebody has just invented a television set that shows pictures in color. We simply *must* have one." And lo, in the light of such heartfelt necessity, a color TV set was purchased.

A few years later still the same son came home from college, saying, "Somebody has just invented a rotary engine that is quieter and more efficient than the old piston jobs. We simply *must* have one." And lo, in the light of such heartfelt necessity, a Mazda was purchased to replace the Ford.

MORAL: *Invention is the mother of necessity.*

HOW TO CLEANSE THE TEMPLE: TWO VERSIONS

THE old version (which is true) went like this:

Once upon a time a man entered the Temple in the capital city. He drove out everybody who was buying and selling in the Temple courts. He even overturned the tables of the moneychangers and the pigeon vendors. He was arrested several days later.

MORAL: *As the defendant put it, "Scripture says, 'My house shall be called a house of prayer,' but you have made it a den of robbers."*

The new version (which is also true) goes like this:

Once upon a time about sixty people (named *Berrigan et al.*) entered a temple in the capital city called the White House. They did not drive out anybody who was taping in the temple courts. They did not even overturn the tables of the "plumbers" or the stool pigeons. All they did was kneel down and pray that the people working in the temple might have a change of heart. They were arrested several minutes later.

MORAL No. 1: *Arresting techniques have become more efficient over the centuries.*

MORAL No. 2: *As the occupant of the latter temple might have put it, "My house has been called a den of robbers, but you have made it a house of prayer."*

THREE LESSONS FOR THE CHURCH TODAY: VARIATIONS ON PROVERBS 29:18 (KJV)

1. Once upon a time there was a group of people who were drawn to one another by virtue of their shared commitment to a vision of what the human community under God might be, believing that they could witness more effectively as a group than as individuals.

MORAL: *Where there is a vision, the people parish.*

2. Later on, the same parish structures that had initially bound them together began to seem oppressively constricting. All began to go their separate ways, heedless of the corporate commitments that had once drawn them together.

MORAL: *Where there is no parish, the people fission.*

3. Soon there were but a handful, and even they drifted apart until finally no one was left who could remember why it had all once seemed so important.

MORAL: *Where there is no people, the vision perishes.*

A TELLING TALE OF TENURE

ONCE upon a time there was a young instructor who wanted to get on the tenure track. So for three years he closed himself off from his students and Revised His Thesis For Publication. This got him a promotion to Ass. Prof. (Assistant Professor). He next isolated himself from his family for four summers running to Assemble The Results Of His Recent Research In Publishable Form. This got him a promotion to Ass. Prof. (Associate Professor). He next got a two-year fellowship (renewable for a third year) to study abroad and Write A Work Of Original Scholarship. This got him a promotion to Full Prof. (Full Professor) and gave him tenure. He was only forty-five. He had arrived.

All was well save for one small shortcoming: he had

never learned how to teach, and no students would take his courses.

The next year he was appointed Dean.

MORAL: *Too many books spoil the prof.*

THE PERILS OF IMBIBING:
A CAUTIONARY TALE FOR CHILDREN

ONCE there was a young woman who had determined to Make It In The World Of Men. She studied hard, competed fiercely, and thus knifed her way toward the top.

Realizing the numbing effect on the brain of even the slightest quantity of alcohol, she very wisely eschewed all intoxicating beverages, until one fine April evening when, on a dare from a young man desirous of having her job, she took a sip from a friend's mug of beer.

That single swallow emboldened her to escalate to wine, from which it was only a short cruise to vermouth, gin, bourbon, scotch, and crème de menthe.

As a result, she lost her cutting edge and fell off the upwardly mobile track.

MORAL: *One swallow doesn't make a summer, but it often leads to a fall.*

A Non-Prose Section

*(So described in deference to those who are
fastidious about the use of the word "Poetry")*

REFLECTIONS ON RECENT BOOK
TITLES,
IN A VARIETY OF STYLES

*

To ask *Whatever Became of Sin?*
Is Menninger's query: just where has sin been?
And no matter how preachers may try to ignore it,
It's perfectly clear that Menninger's for it.

**

Time and Myth by John S. Dunne
Is serious reading, hardly fun.
He deals with life and death so well,
When Dunne is done you've been through hell—
But soon in purgatory rest
And then resume the heav'nly quest.

***

Widen the Prison Gates: Writings from Jails
Is a Philip Berrigan barb that impales
Not only J. Edgar and false charges mounted
But all of the timid who wouldn't be counted

And muted their voices "to be more effective"
While Philip was writing his holy invective.
The barb carries judgment, yet (how like a dove!)
It's a barb that impales, but impales out of love.

****

*An Ethic for Christians
and Other Aliens in a Strange Land*
Is a book title that can be dealt with poetically only by
　resorting to the type of rhythm that a reading
　of Ogden Nash used to demand.
The author William Stringfellow
Is not the sort of person you would call a "Hail fellow
Well met" if you looked him in the eye,
Because he was 50 percent of the Block Island Two that
　protected Daniel Berrigan until he was busted by
　the F.B.I.
He writes about the Book of Revelation apocalyptically,
But the message is straightforward and blunt and threat-
　ening and Biblical and hopeful because it is never
　presented elliptically.

*****

Deloria's book called *God Is Red*
Brings things to a head.
In the face of which it must be said:
Better red than dead.

******

Pedagogy of the Oppressed

Is Paulo Freire at his best.
(The style contains a lot of convolution
But the substance is the stuff of revolution.)

113

LIMERICKS FOR THE LITERATI

CREATIVE CATHOLICISM CONFIRMED THROUGH CONFLICT

A *peritus* named Gregory Baum
Writes books that explode like a bomb-
 shell among the R.C.'s,
 Forcing them to their knees,
Where they learn that Baum's bombs are a balm.

OPIATE OF THE PEOPLE (?)

Some scoffers of Marxism moch
All the fellow trav'lers whose toch
 Would religion deny—
 To which we reply,
If you can't stand Karl Marx, try Ernst Bloch.

THE WORLD: AN EXEGESIS OF THE ELEVENTH THESIS AGAINST FEUERBACH

Philosophers try to arrange it,
Theologs seem to derange it.
 But in our catechesis
 Karl Marx has a thesis:
It's much more important to change it.

THEOLOGY TAILOR-MADE

Jim Cone is persuasively dressed,
His *dashikis* are always the best.
 The evil is lesser
 When he goes to o-pressor
To see that his pants are o-pressed.

Scots Episcopalians

The Anglicans north of the Tweed
Are such an anomalous breed.
  In a land Presbyter'an
  It just ain't God-fearin'
For them to be *chanting* the creed.

David Lotz, Professor of Church History

In the midst of immediate strife,
Dave Lotz lives a scholarly life.
  Though he looks to the rear,
  His wife's vision is clear—
No pillar of salt this Lotz' wife.

Philosophical Theology

Most theologs strongly endorse
A clear philosophical course;
  From a sure, solid footing
  They now dream of putting
Descartes . . . before . . . the horse.

Three on Paul

(1) *A Lay Catholic Reaction*

According to *Our Sunday Missal*
Paul wrote the Ephesian epistle.
  The scholars who doubt it
  List Paul's works without it,
And cause Fr. Murphy to bristle.

(2) *Paul on Sin*

If you seek a deep mind, look at Paul's,
Though his view of truth frequently palls
    On the folks from outside
    And his comments on pride
Treat the Fall with a gall that appalls.

(3) *Saul/Paul*

The act of conversion, we've reckoned,
Is slow for the persons thus beckoned.
    But the road to Damascus
    (In case you should ask us)
Was a place where it took but a second.

LINES COMPOSED LONG AFTER BULTMANN

Come, now, let us offer libation
To a new existential creation:
    De-myth-ol-o-gizing
    Leads to a surprising
Dehermeneutologization.

OWED TO BULTMANN

(May be sung to the tune of "Reuben, Reuben, I've Been Thinking")

CHORUS:

Rudolf, Rudolf, we've been thinking
What a mixed-up world 'twould be,

If our faith were transformed into
Existentiality.

Solo:

Rudolf, Rudolf, what a pity,
If our frankincense and myrrh,
Were dissolved by categories
Drawn from Martin Heidegger.

Rudolf, Rudolf, you have shown us,
That the past must be right here,
And the future is the present—
From there on, the rest is clear.

Rudolf, Rudolf, we believe you,
Heaven here on earth must dwell,
Purgatory's gone to limbo—
Rudolf, where the hell is hell?

Rudolf, Rudolf, we determine
What our fate on earth shall be,
Since you gave us free decision
With your anthropology.

Chorus:

Rudolf, Rudolf, we're committed,
Your approach will see us through,
Rudolf, Rudolf, we're committed,
On-ly we don't know what to.

HEAD OF SISTERS OF LORETTO "RETIRES"

> Sr. Mary Luke Tobin, head of the Sisters of Loretto during its time of "modernization" after Vatican II, has formally retired as head of the order. During her years of leadership, the order emerged (as one sister said, not for attribution) "out of the Catholic ghetto and into the world."
>
> —*News item*

SISTER MARY LUKE RETIRES? NO WAY . . .

(With apologies to Ogden Nash)

ONE of the significant things these days about having
    been head of the Sisters of Loretto
Is how appropriate it is that the word almost rhymes
    with *aggiornametto.*
For when we think of *aggiornamento* (and Lorento) it is
    no fluke
That we immediately think of Sister Mary Luke.
When she and Sister Ann White, S.L., invaded St. Peter's
    as almost the only women in a Vatican Council of
    over 2,000 bishops (male), the authorities thought
    that it would be easy to cope with a 2,000 to 2 ratio,
    only there was in their calculations this slight catch:
That it turned out to be an even match.
And if the Curia thought that Sister Mary Luke would
    remain obscurely docile,
It just goes to show how little they understood her con-
    ception of what it means to be an apostle.
For in ways that cover the possibilities of reform,

renewal, adaptability, worldly apostolate, contemplation, learning, draft board "visitation," the education of bishops, civil disobedience, and other things of the widest possible range,

She has clearly known how to relate continuity and change.

And when she is pressing the church about how the religious orders are to establish reforming guidelines,

She is not satisfied with a slight concession on the height of the sisters' hemlines.

The women who think it is far out and avant-garde and a threat to the whole fabric of our society to be associated with Women's Liberation

Should take Sister Mary Luke into consideration.

For her accomplishments show that if you work hard enough, pray long enough, size up your opposition, rally your supporters, fight sexism wherever it appears, and plan your tactics with sufficient care and divine help (it doesn't really matter in what order you list 'em),

You can still bring about change within the system.

With that kind of record behind her, she will surely (one day) find the heavenly host most anxious to meet her;

But with Sister Mary Luke on hand to rearrange the angelic structures and the celestial appointments, one can only say in terms of friendly admonition, "Be on your guard, St. Peter."

Miscellany
(Things That Didn't Fit Anywhere Else
but Obviously Couldn't Be Left Out)

E PLURIBUS MARTY[1]

> Martin E. Marty, professor of the history of modern Christianity at the University of Chicago, is author of *Righteous Empire,* and, most recently, *Turning East.*
> —*Designation in* The New York Times Book Review, *March 12, p. 15.*

THAT stolid exemplar of modern "investigative reporting," *The New York Times,* likes to explode its journalistic bombs inconspicuously. Whereas the more vulgar *Washington Post* tends to make front-page headlines out of its discoveries of collusion in high places, *The Times* buries its scandalous discoveries discreetly within the cavernous bowels of its Sunday edition—on page 15 of the *Book Review,* for example.

Some months ago, prior to the statement quoted above, *The Times* printed a review of a book called *Turning East,* which its reviewer (following apparently unimpeachable information obtained from the publisher of the book) attributed to an author named "Harvey Cox." An investigative specialist, less naïve than the reviewer, noted the curious repetition of initials ("*H*arvey *C*ox" of

---

[1] One of the best.

"*H*arvard *C*ollege") and suspected a pseudonym. Immediately *The Times* assigned an investigative reporting team to pursue the matter with (as *The Times's* directive put it) "utmost discretion." Gradually it became apparent that more was going on in the writing of religious (or, as the trade says, "inspirational") literature than met the eye, and that a skillfully contrived net of authorial deceit, spun over many years, was about to come apart.

Stylistic comparative studies of the works of "Harvey Cox" were undertaken in relation to the writings of other prolific authors on the religious scene. A propensity for compulsive religious writing emerged as a syndrome marking a number of best-selling authors, among them Michael Novak, Andrew Greeley, and Martin Marty. While Novak's corporeality has long been established, it had been widely hinted that there was no such person as "Andrew Greeley" and that "he" was in fact a syndicate of writers—a sociologist who produced meticulously documented surveys with charts, a popular columnist who wrote widely on everything under the sun, and a group of authors who produced two or three best-selling books a year dealing with the problems of being a twentieth-century Catholic. Query: if "Andrew Greeley" was in fact a team, was it possible that "Harvey Cox" was other than "he" appeared to be?

Evidence began to mount that Martin Marty had a lacuna of thirty unaccounted-for minutes each day of his life as professordeanauthoreditorlecturercolumnist-trendspotterhusbandfatherandLutheran. Feeding this information into a computer, *The Times*'s investigative reporting team discovered that if he chose, Marty could produce out of those cumulative thirty minutes a day any number of books that could be published pseudonymously, thus relieving him of the charge by professional colleagues that he was writing too much.

Such, indeed, turned out to be the case. *The Secular City*, it was discovered, was actually a veiled description by Marty of what it is like to live and work in Chicago. *The Feast of Fools* was a carefully reasoned modern apologia for the Lutheran doctrine of consubstantiation, while *The Seduction of the Spirit* was an attack on chiliastic movements that had threatened seventeenth-century Lutheranism. *Turning East*, the latest production and the one referred to in the above excerpt from *The Times*, was a travel diary Marty had kept of his trips from Chicago to Pittsburgh, Youngstown, Philadelphia, Hartford, Bangor, and Watervliet, N.Y., as from time to time he forsook the city with which for so many years he had had a love-hate relationship.

Besides achieving a truer measure of Marty's actual literary output, *The Times*'s team got new insight into his tactical shrewdness. To promote the sale of his pseudonymous writings, he would arrange for attention to be given to them in *The Christian Century*, a small midwestern Christian house organ on the staff of which Marty serves as part-time editor. On one occasion he even broke into the pages of *Christianity and Crisis* with an "Open Letter to Harvey Cox," giving "Cox" avuncular advice about recovering his Baptist roots—a piece which (as we now know) could more honestly have been entitled "Conversation with Myself."

It became clear, in other words, that "Cox" was the alter ego by means of which Marty kept his fantasy life in touch with reality. Marty was the Lutheran, "Cox" the Baptist; Marty was the establishment spokesperson, "Cox" the renegade social activist; Marty was the historian, "Cox" the contemporary; Marty was the proper Midwesterner, "Cox" the improper Bostonian; Marty was the proprietor of a shaven pate and a balding chin, "Cox" the possessor of a scraggly beard and a full head of hair.

In the meantime, what of "Harvey Cox"? Did he, or did he not, exist? It became clear to Marty that if there were no "Harvey Cox" it would be necessary to invent him. So Marty cleverly arranged for an individual assuming that name to be seen from time to time around Harvard Square, but also to be absent for long periods of time in places like "Cuernavaca" or "Colombia" or "Colorado" (the ongoing repetition of the "C-" syndrome is worth remarking). Marty himself often appeared in public places sporting a false beard and hairpiece, giving trendy talks and collecting "Cox's" honoraria, after which he would double back to the University of Chicago to sit in on oral examinations about obscure eighteenth-century historians.

All this and more *The Times* uncovered. Aware, however, of the peculiar sensibilities of the religious community, and less than eager to have an ecclesiastical Watergate on its hands, it chose to unveil its conclusions discreetly and modestly, leaving it to those with sharp eyes to put the facts together. Hence the almost casual attribution to Marty, cited above, of the book the public thought all the time was authored by "Cox."

Even this, however, is not the full story. Having discovered that Marty and "Andrew Greeley" both live in "Chicago" (which may itself be a pseudonym for something it would be impossible to invent), the team is pursuing leads suggesting that "Andrew Greeley" may be yet another pseudonym employed by Marty, the better to cover his tracks. (The fact that "Greeley" has recently moved to Arizona suggests that the trail is getting hot.) It is known that Marty can write from 250 to 750 words a minute, depending on the weather. Computer-wise (as they say in the trade), it is mathematically possible that Marty's cumulative thirty minutes per day could account for even the stream of writings the public at present attributes to "Greeley."

What could be more fitting? If one side of the Lutheran Marty yearns for the Baptist free-church tradition, might there not be another side of Marty yearning for the structured life of modern Catholicism, so winsomely depicted in the writings of "Andrew Greeley"? Indeed, if Marty-"Cox" has produced a book called *Turning East*, may we not look forward to a Marty-"Greeley" book called *Go West, Young Man?*

THE NEW LOGIC[1]

BLIND MAN HELPS CENSOR
ROCKLAND COUNTY FILMS
    —*Headline in* The New York Times

HERE is a startling new logic that, if extended to other fields, could revolutionize the nature and direction of our American culture. If the Rockland County approach to social change should sweep the country, we can begin to expect headlines like the following:

BERRIGAN BROTHERS TO HEAD
PENTAGON BUDGET ADVISORY STAFF

"New Input Needed,"

---

[1]By methods of redaction criticism of the original text, coupled with the known demise of several of the persons mentioned below, it can be established that the headlines cited were conceived in the late fall of 1973. [Ed.]

Generals Concede
Catonsville Experience in Napalm Manufacture
Cited as Reason for Choice

Headship of AATS Goes to Charles Dillon (Casey) Stengel

Indicating that his prose sounds as if it had been inspired by theology textbooks, the Board of Directors of the American Association of Theological Schools (AATS) announced today that C. Dillon Stengel would head the AAAS for the next quadrennium. Reached for comment at his Glendale bank, Stengel responded, "It's of that fella out centerfield where we don't want base stealing much more and them is the facts production-wise," interpreted by this reporter to be Mr. Stengel's exegesis of the Yahwist version of the Creation story.

Hugh Hefner Assumes Editorship of *Ms.*

Promising that his appointment would bring "a fresh perspective" to the magazine, Pat Carbine announced today that Hugh Hefner would supervise editorial content of *Ms.* beginning with the next issue. Mr. Hefner announced simultaneously that the centerfold of the magazine (to be renamed *Playperson*) would feature Sal Bando, Esq., peripatetic major-league third baseman.

Maharaj Ji Will Head Geriatric Institute

The Board of Directors today released information that the leadership of the Geriatric Institute of Palm Beach has been offered to Maharaj Ji, a 15-year-old evangelist from India. "He really turns the inmates on," was the comment of the 84-year-old former director.

Hans Küng to Head Papal Commission
for Reform of Curia

ROME—Citing the need "to complete the evolutionary restructuring of the papal court along the lines laid down by Vatican II," the pope announced today that he had personally selected Prof. Dr. Dr. Hans Küng of Tübingen to conduct a thorough investigation of past curial procedures, particularly in the area of the establishment of doctrinal orthodoxy, as a basis for recommending changes. "We will feel Ourself morally bound to accept his proposals for the future," the Holy Father concluded.

BILLY GRAHAM TO HEAD
BLACK MUSLIMS

. . . Elijah Muhammad, in announcing the appointment of Mr. Graham today, remarked, "It's part of our new affirmative action program."

FIRST THE GOOD NEWS . . .
THEN THE GOOD NEWS

Dr. Norman Vincent Peale . . . is about to launch a radio program accentuating the positive side of the news. In a

Monday-to-Friday series of 90-second spots, underwritten by ITT [International Telephone and Telegraph Corporation] as a public service and distributed free to stations around the U.S., Peale will report on good deeds, heroic acts, and other upbeat events. "These acts are many times more prevalent than the constant reports of violence, greed, and corruption we hear all the time," Peale maintains.

—Newsweek, *issue appearing on the newsstands on March 21*

TWO AT ITT ACCUSED OF PERJURY ON CHILE

U.S. Indicates No Criminal Charges Will Be Brought Against Geneen

WASHINGTON, March 20—The Justice Department today charged two officials of the International Telephone and Telegraph Corporation with a total of 12 felony offenses, all of them stemming from their testimony to a Senate subcommittee about the company's involvement in the 1970 presidential election in Chile. . . .

The Department indicated that it did not intend to bring criminal charges against Harold S. Geneen, ITT's chairman, who was also being investigated because of testimony he gave at those same 1973 hearings.

—The New York Times, *March 21 (the same day)*

HERE is a nice dilemma for Dr. Peale. His sponsor, ITT, has underwritten him to tell us about upbeat events that counteract constant reports of "greed and corruption." But the actions taken against ITT are so full of good news that it will be hard for him to fit everything into a 90-second spot. He needs help. Here is a proposed format, full rights to which I generously bequeath to ITT and its new newscaster.

ANNOUNCER *(after fade-in and fade-out of "Brighten the Corner Where You Are," sung by the Collegiate Chorale)*: International Telephone and Telegraph Corporation agrees with Dr. Norman Vincent Peale that we hear too much these days about "violence, greed, and corruption." Good deeds and heroic acts take place too, and ITT believes we should concentrate on them. We are therefore donating 90 seconds each day so that Dr. Peale can bring us the positive side of the news. These programs are provided free to U.S. radio stations by ITT. And now . . . *live* from New York . . . Dr. . . . Norman . . . Vincent . . . Peale!

DR. PEALE: Good morning, ladies and gentlemen, this is Norman Vincent Peale bringing you the good deeds, the heroic acts, the upbeat events we tend to overlook in the midst of violence, greed, and corruption.

Our sponsor, ITT, provides the occasion for today's good news. Let us not dwell on charges that ITT's "greed and corruption" brought "violence" to Chile. That would be negativism. Let us rather laud the courage of our fine Justice Department for moving in to indict high-level ITT officials. It would have been easy for the Justice Department to vacillate, to waffle, to accept bribes. Isn't it happy news that our Government officials moved fearlessly, despite what must have been strong pressures from our sponsor? Let us rejoice that justice *is* done without favoritism, that there still *is* integrity in Washington.

I know that many of you who are listening are board chairmen, and find yourselves so weighed down with responsibility that you become anxious and distraught. If officials of *your* corporation should be charged with felony offenses, wouldn't you be fearful that you too might be indicted? Well, all of you board chairmen can erase such negative thoughts. For today's positive side of the news is that Harold S. Geneen, chairman of ITT, will not be further investigated, even though 12 felony offenses are being charged against high-up officials of his corporation.

It is frequently said by negative thinkers that the sponsors "manage" the news, dictate what may be said on the air, censor all attempts to get at any truth that might hurt them. But consider the positive side of the news: ITT, rather than resorting to "cover-ups," is actually sponsoring a broadcast that exposes its own alleged moral shortcomings to the American people, and furthermore . . .

ANNOUNCER (*cutting in crisply*): Ladies and gentlemen, we are sorry to interrupt this broadcast on the positive side of the news, sponsored by ITT and featuring Dr. Norman Vincent Peale. Due to a regrettable misunderstanding between Dr. Peale and the sponsor, the broadcast today was done "live." ITT's new policy, in order to ensure uniformity of production standards, is that future broadcasts will be taped well in advance at ITT's own private studios and shipped to cooperating stations directly. Should you wish further information about future transcribed programs by Dr. Peale featuring the positive side of the news, please contact the Public Relations Department of ITT.

THEOLOGICAL VENERY; OR,
A SYNECDOCHE OF METAPHORS

"VENERY" isn't what you think it is.

The dictionary defines "venery" as "(*archaic*) the art or

practice of hunting," or "*(archaic)* the indulgence of sexual desire." The dictionary doesn't admit it, but there is a better, loftier meaning. Venery is *really* an artful sort of word game, the object of which is to invent a striking phrase—poetic or punsterish—to describe a collectivity. The trick is to make an unexpected noun out of some characteristic of the object to be collectivized ("a *complacency of bankers*") or of the collectivity itself ("a *string of ponies*"). James Lipton, in *An Exaltation of Larks* (New York: Grossman Publishers)—the very title of which is an example of venery at its best—has provided hundreds of examples of venery, but he has unaccountably overlooked the rich resources to be found in such fields as theology, ecclesiology, church history, and canon law.

It was our original intention to classify and categorize various examples of venery, e.g., those that were basically theological ("a kennel of dogmatists"), those belonging to historical or denominational categories ("a rack of Inquisitors," "an assurance of Calvinists"), those overladen with value judgments ("a surfeit of bishops"), those depending on subtle wordplay ("a bag of vadgetas"), those already timeworn ("a communion of saints"), those taken from such related fields as physics ("a breed of reactors"), not to mention those that were clearly borderline ("a gloss o'lalia").

However, as with any infant science, there is a danger of premature classification, likely to freeze the subject matter in ways that make later definitive classification more difficult precisely as it becomes more necessary. In keeping with this principle, therefore, we deliberately offer a hodgepodge, hoping that while the truly inspired examples will endure, those offerings that strain too much for effect will fall by the wayside, so that out of it all, appropriate and lasting classifications will emerge, slowly and gradually, as the new discipline matures and as the material thus uncovered works its way carefully into our incurably systematic minds. (NOTE: In this chauvinistic age, it is important to record that the contributions below are the product of a group we can identify as "Hereticus et ux.")

a swish of nuns (archaic; now in process of being replaced by:)
an agitation of sisters
a drawerful of bureaucrats
a meticulation of theologians
a chancery of monsignori
a ms. of feminists
a hassle of activists
a freeze of traditionalists
a pyre of heretics (or, more positively:)
a blaze of martyrs
an annoyance of prophets
a *praxis* of liberationists
a dialectic of Hegelians
a chant of liturgists
a flurry of angels (or:)
a rumor of angels (thanks to P. Berger)
a rash of edicts
a pen of encyclicals
a nihil of obstats
a joy of sects
an immersion of Baptists
a glut of hedonists
a rod of judgments
a precision of creeds
a haberdash of miters
a sola of Scriptures
a defiance of atheists
a chaos of Catholics (post-Vatican II)

a purr of catechists
an explosion of canonists
a concurrence of ecumenists
a convenience of synthesists (or, alternatively:)
a montage of synthesists
a situation of ethicists
a remonstrance of anathemas
a catchall of pronouncements
a celebration of mysteries
a niggling of legalists
a fragmentation of schismatics
a vacillation of contextualists
a tremor of millenarians
a stand of Lutherans
a huddle of Congregationalists
a sensation of kerygmatics
an anarchy of charismatics
a scratch of scribes
a straining of casuists
a whirl of dervishes
a grimace of cynics
a trio of Synoptics
a cackle of clerics
a garnish of gnostics
a patrimony of chauvinists
a shattering of iconoclasts
a tension of antagonists
a confusion of tongues
a closet of gays (archaic)
an initiative of Pelagians
a frustration of administrators
a summation of Thomists
a stridency of Jansenists
a karload of Barthians
a guilt of perfectionists

a scrupulosity of confessants
a metamorphosis of transubstantiationalists

Your turn . . .

Appendix

THEOLOGICAL GAMESMANSHIP;
OR,
DISPOSING OF LIBERATION
THEOLOGY
IN EIGHT EASY LESSONS[1]

THE increasing attention being given to so-called "liberation theology" is worrisome. All kinds of people who ought to know better see it as a recovery of the Christian message in Asia, Africa, and Latin America that is transforming lives, bringing dead churches to life again, making dictators tremble, and demonstrating that the old faith can still have power. Anytime contemporary Christians begin to side with the poor, forsaking Christianity's historic alliance with privilege and affluence, a counter-offense must be mounted.

Ordinarily I would ignore the movement, fearing that

---

[1]One of the keys to successful Gamesmanship is the inclusion of multitudes of footnotes to indicate that one is A Real Scholar. In the present instance, however, ostensibly as the initiation of a possible Reverse Trend, but chiefly to save money in typesetting, a revolutionary device has been employed: *footnote-style comments have been incorporated within the main body of the text.* A subtle message is thus communicated: It is the academically insecure who need to buttress their published works with footnotes. Those who are really on top of their material will not feel dependent on such ostentatious devices. [Ed.]

if attention is called to it innocent people will be lured into its embrace by the seductive prose and unassuming life-styles of its proponents. But the movement is now firmly launched, and even the bishops are worried about how to contain it. Since liberation theology is now the subject of wide debate, with the world watching, this is hardly a time for craven silence.

I am not above offering help even to bishops, and when I think, in addition, of all the ordinary Christians who wish to keep the present order secure, it seems crucial to provide gambits, ploys, and arguments to dispose of the disturbing impact liberation theology has already had. Herewith are eight approaches designed to achieve that desirable goal:

1. *Dismiss liberation theology as "only a fad." Better yet, dismiss it as only "the latest fad."* Such a characterization dispels the notion that liberation theology needs to be taken seriously. When the subject is broached, ask, rather eagerly, "What do you suppose will be 'the next fad'?" Recall short-lived "earlier fads," such as the death of God, the secular city, the Zen kick, or whatever else comes to mind.

Take care, however, that your opponents do not internalize the fact that liberation theology is calling for an end to the oppression of the poor, and that since liberation theology is not likely to disappear until the oppression of the poor disappears, it is going to be on the scene a long, long time—long enough, surely, to render the term "fad" irrelevant if not condescending.

2. *Describe liberation theology as "mere reductionism."* (Remember throughout that liberal use of the adjective "mere" is the most potent weapon in our whole arsenal of tricks.) The reductionism can be applied to almost anything "mere" that you choose: (a) mere ethics, (b) mere politics, (c) mere economics, or (d) Marxism/

136

socialism/communism. (In the latter instances, "mere" is unnecessary, since words ending in "-ism" can be discredited almost as easily as words preceded by "mere.")

Take care, however, that your opponents do not actually *read* liberation theology, since they will find it studded with Biblical exegesis, ecclesiological reflection, theological history, essays on spirituality, disturbing references to "following Jesus," and so on. Tell them instead, not to waste their time reading liberation theology, but to take your word for it. Otherwise you will be in trouble.

3. *Accuse liberation theologians of "espousing violence."* Surefire. Who wants to support a position that "espouses violence"? Violence is, after all, un-Christian, the antithesis of the gospel, as we all know so well. Conjure up visions of trigger-happy clerics storing submachine guns in the sacristy, just waiting for orders from the nearest military "secular" revolutionary to whom they long ago secretly swore fealty.

Take care, however, that your opponents do not discover that liberation theology speaks of violence only as a last resort when all else fails, a position in total accord with about 98.6 percent of the rest of the Christian world, since by this criterion all other theologians and theologies (save only the Quakers, the Mennonites, and a few stray individuals named Helder Câmara, Berrigan, and so forth) would likewise be discredited. Do not let them reflect on the fact that the structures of our society are *already violent* and destructive to the poor, long before anyone ever gets around to picking up a rock or a gun.

4. *Point out that liberation theology is "culturally conditioned" and that therefore it does not concern us.* Describe it as a slightly exotic variant on normative theology (i.e., ours), a product of a certain geographical locale ("down there"), able to speak, perhaps, to a few unlettered poor,

but not, consequently, of concern to us. This projects a pleasantly tolerant live-and-let-live attitude ("We have our theology, they have theirs") that conveniently, and not so incidentally, gets us off the hook of having to take the position seriously.

Take care, however, that your opponents do not discover that their own theology is just as much culturally conditioned—informed by North American, rather than South American, *mores;* done out of affluence rather than poverty; employing capitalist rather than socialist assumptions; intended to buttress rather than challenge the status quo. Be particularly careful to suppress any suggestion that South American poverty might be due to North American political, economic, and military domination of that continent, since this *would* force them to take it seriously.

5. *Stress the fact that liberation theology's use of the Bible is "highly selective."* (NOTE: Do not employ this argument in conjunction with the argument about "reductionism," No. 2 above, since the two are mutually exclusive—a fact someone might notice and use against you.) Point out how frequently and one-sidedly liberation theologians revert to "the same old passages": the exodus story, Jer. 22:13–16, Isa. 58:6–7, Luke 1:46–55, Luke 4:16–30 (with an assist from Isaiah 61), Matt. 25:31–46, and so on. Complain, in a voice carefully modulated between wistfulness and bitterness: "Whatever happened to the rest of the canon?"

Take care, however, that your opponents do not discover how typical the above passages are of the *rest* of Scripture. Especially thwart the counterargument that the opponents themselves employ a collection of verses carefully selected from the whole of Scripture ("The poor you have always with you," is a particular favorite), lest someone turn on them and say, very tellingly if not too originally, (in a voice carefully modulated between wistfulness and bitterness): "Whatever happened to the rest of the canon?"

6. *Accuse liberation theology of demanding that the church "take sides."* It is well known, of course, that the church, in order to minister to *all* of its constituents, must refrain from taking sides, lest it seem concerned with only a portion of humanity (the poor), and cut itself off from the others (us) who likewise need to hear the salvific message.

Take care, however, that your opponents do not discover that neutrality is actually impossible. "Not to take sides" is, as liberation theologians have an annoying way of reminding us, to take sides with the status quo. Keep your opponents oblivious of the fact that their restiveness in the face of liberation theology may even be due to the fact that their own well-being is threatened by liberation theology's unambiguous identification with the poor, a strata of society with whom your opponents are unlikely to be closely identified.

7. *If things are going really badly, resort to the charge that liberation theology is "the product of Marxist analysis."* This riposte can pull almost any chestnut out of any fire. Note that the argument is not simply an example of the "reductionism" argument (see No. 2, above) but can stand on its own; no matter how ample may be the Christian or Biblical dimensions of liberation theology, if it can be called "Marxist" that alone will suffice to demolish it. Added beauty of the gambit: one need not define the word "Marxist." One need only utter it.

Take care, however, that your opponents are not confronted by the following response: "Let us first ask whether the analysis is *true,* rather than ask who propounded it. If it is true, then who propounded it is a matter of secondary importance. If it is not true, then whoever propounded it is already discredited."

8. *If all else fails, or there simply isn't enough time, employ the basic principle for dealing with a position difficult to refute: co-opt it.* Suggest that liberation theology is good as far as it goes but that it doesn't go far enough, e.g.: "It's all very well to talk about political and economic liberation, but what about *spiritual* liberation? Isn't that the really important thing as far as Christians are concerned?" Refer to your own more ample statement as *"authentic* liberation theology," in contrast to "distorted" or "inadequately developed" liberation theology, or even (see the first sentence of this essay) "so-called" liberation theology. Remind your opponents that poverty is not just a misfortune to those without material possessions, but that *all* of us are poor, poor in the things that really count, i.e., the deep spiritual values whose absence renders all human life meaningless. There is, of course, just enough truth in these observations to enable their proponents to spend a lifetime pondering them so that they will never have to deal with liberation from economic or political injustice. The best co-optation, therefore, is to say, *as soon as the subject of liberation theology is raised,* "But we're *all* oppressed."

Take care, however, that your opponents never discover that there is a significant distinction between those who say, "I'm so oppressed by overwork that I compensate by overeating and have this weight problem," and those who say, "I'm so oppressed by lack of work that I can't buy food for my children to eat and we are all starving to death."

Keeping that distinction blurred is the surest way to dispose of liberation theology.

Index of Names, Places, Ideas, Themes, Leftovers

NAMES

Alinsky, Saul, 85
Allen, Woody, 16
Aristotle, 16
Augustine, St., 28–29, 89
Avila, Teresa of, 89
Baggins, Frodo, 263–292
Baillie, Donald, 85
Baillie, John, 85
Balthasar, Hans Urs von, 85
Barth, Karl, 35, 85
Baum, Gregory, 114
Bennett, John, 85
Berdyaev, Nicolas, 85
Berger, Peter, 131
Berrigans, 53, 109, 112–113, 124, 137
Blake, Eugene Carson, 71, 88
Bloch, Ernst, 16, 114
Bonhoeffer, Dietrich, 85
Borovoi, Protopresbyter, 71
Boyle, Eugene, 91–94
Boyle, Robert, 91
Brightman, Edgar, 85
Brown, Petermarkalisontom,
    passim
Brown, Rap, 24
Brown, Sydney, 131, and passim
Buber, Martin, 55, 85
Bucer, Martin, See
    Buber, Martin
Bulgakov, Sergei, 85
Bultmann, Rudolf, 85, 87, 116–117

Bunyan, John, 34
Buri, Fritz, 85
Calvin, John, 89
Câmara, Dom Helder, 137
Canterbury, Anselm of, 13, 31, 89
Claus, Santa, 11–19
Climacus, Johannes, 56–57
Cone, James, 114
Cox, Harvey, 61, 120–124
Culpa, O. Felix, 5
Dante, Immortal, 18
Deloria, Vine, 113
Descartes, René, 16, 115
Driver, Tom, 84
Eck, Johann, 65
Feuerbach, Ludwig, 114
Forstman, H. Jackson, 61, 89
Freire, Paulo, 113
Fry, John, 88
Gandalf, 263–292
Gilkey, Langdon, 61
Graham, Billy, 126
Greeley, Andrew, 121–124
Handy Robert T., 57
Hegel, G. W. F., 55, 56, 131
Homans, Jennifer, 71n
't Hooft, W. A. Visser, 56, 57, 71
Iscariot, Judas, 49
ITT, 127–129
James, William, 28
Kant, Immanuel, 12–13

PLACES

IDEAS, THEMES, LEFTOVERS

THE EDITOR, Robert McAfee Brown, taught systematic theology at Union Theological Seminary from 1953 to 1962, moved to Stanford University ("from Jerusalem to Athens") to teach religious studies, moved back to Union in 1976 ("from Athens to Jerusalem") to teach practical theology, and moved to Pacific School of Religion in 1979 ("from 10027 to 94709") to teach theology and ethics. Disdaining charges that he cannot hold down a job, he replies that "theology should always be on the move."

He is also the editor of *The Collect'd Writings of St. Hereticus* (a previously published companion to the present volume), which he humbly describes as "a significant attempt to keep theologians humble." A number of his other writings have been remaindered—significant testimony to the fact that theologians are kept humble whether they desire it or not.